SAVE AND
INVEST
WITH
ALVIN HALL

ALSO BY ALVIN HALL

Money For Life
Winning With Shares
Your Money or Your Life
What Not to Spend
You and Your Money

SAVE AND
INVEST
WITH
ALVIN HALL

HODDER &
STOUGHTON

To Josephine
for 'bustin' my chops' about saving
and
To Vicki
for her example-setting prudent ways
in handling money

Copyright © 2006 by Alvin Hall

First published in Great Britain in 2006 by Hodder & Stoughton
A division of Hodder Headline

The right of Alvin Hall to be identified as the Author
of the Work has been asserted by him in accordance
with the Copyright, Designs and Patents Act 1988.

A Hodder & Stoughton Book

1

A CIP catalogue record for this title is available from the British Library

ISBN 0 340 83359 9

Typeset in Berkeley Old Style by Hewer Text UK Ltd, Edinburgh
Printed and bound by Clays Ltd, St Ives plc;

Hodder Headline's policy is to use papers that are natural, renewable
and recyclable products and made from wood grown in sustainable
forests. The logging and manufacturing processes are expected to
conform to the environmental regulations of the country of origin.

Hodder & Stoughton Ltd
A division of Hodder Headline
338 Euston Road
London NW1 3BH

CONTENTS

Acknowledgements

Thanks to the following people for their diligent, thoughtful, and expert work on and contributions to this series of books: Laura Collins (for her brilliant copy editing), Emma Heyworth-Dunn (for her useful initial comments), Helen Coyle (who inherited this project and handled it and me with expert and caring skill, not unlike a midwife), Jonathan Drori (for giving me my first opportunity to do television), Daisy Goodwin (who hired me for *Your Money or Your Life* through which I gained many of the insights in this book), Stephanie Faber (for her expert publicity for my TV show and her on-going encouragement and friendship), Richard Farmbrough (for being my always honest friend and for his sensitive production skills on the first three series of *Your Money or Your Life*), Emma Longhurst (for her great publicity work at Hodder), Vicki McIvor (for her dedication as my agent, protector, adviser, and friend), Robert McKenzie (for being true blue and generous with his knowledge and opinions), Gill Paul (for her initial efforts in helping to shape these books), Sarah Pennells (for her generosity, expertise, and wry sense of humor), Rowena Webb (for believing in my work and always being honest about it), Karl Weber (for being my trusted friend, my moderator, my spiritual inspiration), and, as always, everyone who appeared on *Your Money or Your Life*, *Investing for All with Alvin Hall*, *Save Me, Alvin* and other series I've done. Thanks for making me feel that my work was beneficial. Through these books I hope to share with others my knowledge of the practical strategies, insights, and benefits of handling your finances with focus, discipline, and a little fun. I know that each of you can make your money work in ways that will enable you to achieve some of the things we all desire – a debt-free life, a beautiful home, and the comfort of financial security.

Alvin Hall, London, April 2006

1 | GETTING STARTED IN SAVING

Why Save?

For many people, saving and investing are a bit like dieting and exercising: you've been told you ought to do it, and maybe you even agree, but it's hard to translate that vague sense of obligation, and possibly guilt, into the motivation required to change your behaviour every day. In this book, I want to provide you with practical tools that can help you get past the guilt and focus instead on positive actions that will improve your life (and make you feel better in the process).

Let's start with the two main reasons it's important to save. You'll notice that neither one involves guilt or the old Protestant work ethic. First, saving can prepare you for the ups and downs of life. The habit of saving can ensure that the good things you enjoy won't completely disappear when trouble strikes. What kind of trouble? Consider this list of possibilities:

- There is a recession in your industry and you are made redundant from your job. Or, if you are self-employed, the demand for your services unexpectedly dries up.
- You suffer an illness or injury that makes it impossible for you to work for a year.
- Your spouse or partner dies, or your relationship breaks up.
- Fire, accident or natural disaster damages or destroys your home or your possessions.
- An unexpected illness or pregnancy brings medical bills and a drastic change in lifestyle with new expenses, lower income and possible medical bills.
- Your cooker, fridge, washing machine and central-heating boiler break down at the same time.

If you've never had to face any of these problems, congratulations! You've been very lucky – so far. But as you know, almost everyone experiences one or more of these setbacks at some time in his or her life (just think about your family and friends). In a bad year, two or three may strike at once. If you're prepared, you can bounce back with minimal long-term damage. If you're not, it may take decades to free yourself from the financial burden.

To cover you in such crises, I recommend that you accumulate at least three months of your take-home salary in an easily accessible, risk-free savings account. If you are a homeowner, have children or other dependents, or are self-employed, six months' income would be a safer figure. Call this your 'lifeboat account', since it's designed to carry you to safety in case of emergency. Creating this lifeboat is your first reason to save, and it's an eminently practical (even selfish) one.

The second reason is more pleasant to contemplate: saving is a pathway to making your dreams come true. What kind of dreams? Here's another, very different, list:

- You buy a beautiful house, or renovate and expand your current dwelling to transform it into the home of your dreams.
- You take several months off from work to travel round the world, pursue a hobby, craft or art, or just rediscover the joys of leisure.
- You are able to retire from work with a comfortable lifestyle you know you can enjoy for the rest of your life.
- Your child is able to enjoy a first-rate university education that launches him or her into a successful career.
- You buy or start a business of your own – a restaurant, a shop, a consulting business – and finally get the chance to be your own boss.

Maybe you have other dreams that are different from these, dreams you may assume can never really come true. But today's dreams can become tomorrow's reality, provided you start saving *now* to make it happen.

Saving, Investing and Speculating

The three activities named above look similar, and people often confuse them. In fact, they're quite different, and the distinctions among them are important.

Saving is putting away a portion of your current income in a building society account or bank account, or other safe haven where it will grow *with almost no risk*. How is this possible? A governmental safety net is the reason. If a bank or building society in the UK should fail (due to mismanagement, for example), the financial services industry has an independent compensation scheme to reimburse depositors' money up to a maximum of £31,700 (100% of the first £2000 and 90% of the next £33,000). This is why a savings account in a bank or building society is considered so low-risk: the value of your account can only grow, never shrink.

And if you're diligent about saving regularly, the growth of your money can be substantial, thanks to *compound interest*. Interest is the money the bank pays you in return for keeping your funds with them. It's expressed in percentage terms. For example, if you have a savings account that pays 4% interest per annum, that means you'll be paid £4 per year for every £100 in your account. Compounding speeds up the growth of your money. It refers to the interest that is paid *on your interest*. In other words, your money earns money . . . and then the money you've earned begins to earn even more money!

Over time, compound interest has a powerful impact on the amount of saving you accumulate. For example, suppose you were to save £100 per month for the next ten years. If you simply hid the money in your closet, where it earned *no* interest, you'd end up with £12,000, provided an unscrupulous friend or family member doesn't find your stash and spend it first. Not a bad little nest egg. But if you deposited the same amount into a bank account that paid 4% interest, compounded monthly, you'd have £14,694. It's like getting an extra £2,694 'free', just for letting the bank hold it. This is what a combination of a saving habit and compound interest can do for you and your money.

Like saving, *investing* is about putting aside a portion of your income so that it can grow, except that investing is not so risk-free. When you invest, you use your money to purchase a financial instrument like a unit trust, a share or a bond. You can also invest in property. The value of these instruments can increase over time; in fact, often they grow *faster* than the money in a savings account, but this doesn't always happen. Sometimes the value of an investment *falls*, and in some rare cases, you may even lose all of your money. And when that happens, there's no government scheme to bail you out. So before you invest, you need to think about the amount of risk – i.e. the possibility of losing the money you've invested – you are willing to accept in exchange for a potential reward.

This difference means that while everyone should save, not

everyone should invest. You should invest only when you have some *extra* money beyond your lifeboat account. In other words, this is money that you'd like to see grow, but that you can afford to lose in part or in whole without ruining your life.

Later in this book, we'll explain how to invest without taking on excessive risk. For many people, wise investing has been a route to financial security and even wealth. If you have ambitious dreams you'd like to realise – education for your kids, owning a business or a home, retiring in style – you will want to start investing as soon as you can, so that your money can grow to make those dreams possible.

Finally, there is *speculating*. When you speculate, you use the money you've saved to buy assets that *may* grow in value but that also have a good chance of becoming completely valueless. Buying a painting by a young, unknown artist is an example. There's a chance that someday Mr X will be world-famous, and that collectors in New York, London and Paris will be interested in paying a high price to acquire the work you own to hang on their walls. But it's much more likely that Mr X will remain unknown, and that your painting will never be worth any more than the £250 you paid for it, or perhaps even less if no one wants to buy it.

Speculation, then, is ultra high risk, more akin to gambling on lottery tickets or betting on racehorses than investing. For a lucky few, the returns from speculating can be great, but most speculators lose their money. Later, we'll describe the most common forms of speculation, show how they differ from investing and explain why you should probably avoid them altogether, at least from a financial perspective. Go ahead and buy Mr X's painting if you like it, but don't expect the profit to finance your retirement. And if it does, count yourself lucky.

The First Step – Clearing Your Personal Debt

Before you start saving or investing, you must escape from the burden of *personal debt*.

Are you, like millions of other Britons, carrying credit- or store-card balances from month to month? If so, you are probably paying a significant amount of interest on your unpaid balances. Most likely, this is a much higher rate of interest than you can expect to earn from a savings account or an investment plan. Therefore it makes sense to clear your debts before you start to save or invest. Otherwise, it's like pouring water into a bucket with lots of holes in the bottom: the amount you lose each month on the credit-card (or store-card) interest charges will be greater than the amount you can earn in interest on your savings account.

(Notice that I'm talking here about personal or consumer debt – that is, amounts you owe on credit cards, store cards, car loans and personal loans from a bank or building society. A home mortgage is a different matter. Unlike the items you buy with a credit card, a home is a long-term investment, and interest rates on mortgages are usually much lower than the rates on personal loans and credit. I don't recommend, therefore, that you try to pay off your home mortgage before you think about saving or investing.)

Generally speaking, the best approach to getting out of debt is to pay off as much as you can every month. Start with the debt that is charging the *highest* interest rate. This debt is the most expensive one because it is costing you the most to carry each month. Look for the annual percentage rate, or APR, on each credit-card or store-card bill you receive, or phone the lender if you can't locate the figure. Work to pay the debt with the highest APR first, then move down through your other debts, from highest to lowest APR, until you've paid them all off. Depending on the size of the debt hole you have dug for yourself, this process may take a few months or even a few years. You must be diligent and patient. Remember, it takes a lot more discipline to get out of debt than it did to get in.

If your debts are serious and you can't see how you are going to clear them, my book *Get Out of Debt with Alvin Hall* has much more information and can help you create a plan for solving this problem. It's important to stop this needless drain on your income before you work on accumulating money for a saving and investing plan.

Building Your Lifeboat Account

Once you've freed yourself from the burden of consumer debt, you're ready for the next stage in creating a strong financial future – creating the three- to six-month lifeboat account you need for protection against life's unexpected misfortunes.

For many people, the idea of saving this much money seems overwhelming. 'I barely have enough money to pay my bills every month,' they say. 'How on earth can I put away several months' worth of income? It's just not possible.'

I know the feeling. It seemed impossible to me – until I did it. Here are seven proven techniques for saving that thousands and thousands of people have used to make the seemingly impossible, possible – and even easy.

1. *Make saving a habit.* Aim to deposit 10–15% of your monthly income into a savings account until you've got your three-month cushion in place. If you target 10%, for example, it would take 30 months to stockpile 3 months' take-home pay (or 60 months for 6 months' take-home pay). If you can't manage 10%, just put aside whatever you can – £100, £50, even £20. The key is to make saving a regular habit. As with eating a proper diet, exercising, or even brushing your teeth, once you become accustomed to a particular activity, it's easy to continue.

2. *Save first.* Set up a direct debit so that the money you want to save is transferred out of your current account and into your

savings account as soon as your salary is paid in and, most importantly, before you've even had a chance to let your spending desire take over. Don't rely on remembering to arrange a transfer every month. Unless you are really disciplined (which most of us are not), there will always be times when you decide you can't afford it or when you just forget (conveniently) to make the transfer. Excuses are easy. Direct debit makes saving automatic and painless, as you will really never miss money if it's never in your pocket to begin with.

3. *Use a different bank for your savings.* Try keeping your emergency savings account in a different bank or building society from your current account or any other accounts you may have. Once it's there, try doing a bit of self-hypnotism and forget that it even exists! This account is not a pot for dipping into when you fancy a new coat, the car needs a fresh set of tyres or there's a special offer on kitchen units at the local B&Q. If you give in to the temptation to use your savings for things like this, you'll be sorry if and when a *real* emergency comes along.

4. *Use a limited-access account.* This is a special kind of bank account that only allows you to make a limited number of withdrawals a year. Most banks and building societies offer such an account, and it can be a handy deterrent for your own less-than-ironclad willpower. And if you must dip into your fund for a true emergency, make sure you replace the money as quickly as possible.

5. *Save rather than spend any extra funds you receive.* To speed up the saving process, you can deposit any end-of-year bonuses, cash gifts, inheritances or windfalls into your savings account. If you get a pay rise at work, increase your regular payments into your savings account by half or all of the increase. You already know that it's possible to live on the amount you've been earning previously, and you are not likely to miss what you've never had. If you've been paying off a bank or car loan, once you make the final payment, start putting the same amount of money – or at the very least half of it – in your savings account. Most people would give in to the temptation to spend that money. Don't. Save it instead!

6. *Tie your saving to your spending.* Each time you spend money on something that is not a necessity, immediately (and I mean *immediately*) deposit the same amount into your savings account. You should not spend the money on a CD, jumper, pair of jeans or anything that you know you don't need if you cannot deposit the money into savings. This strategy not only increases the money going into your savings, but has the additional benefit of curbing the spending that undermines your ability to save.

7. *Sacrifice a habit.* At the beginning of each year, give up something that you do regularly, like buying a latte every morning, buying yourself a piece of clothing or cosmetics each time you get a pay packet, and deposit that money into your savings account. I once did this by giving up buying

coats for two years and then giving up buying shirts for a
year. Each year I make a different sacrifice and put the
money I save into a savings account or investment account.

Does applying self-discipline to your financial life feel difficult
before you've even tried? Are you afraid you'll find it hard to be
so strict with yourself? When I was struggling to create my own
lifeboat account many years ago, I felt the same way at first. I
turned it into a personal challenge, setting monthly and annual
savings targets, then rewarding myself with a treat only when I
achieved them – treats like theatre tickets, a new piece of
clothing I'd coveted, dinner at my favourite restaurant or a
cheap package trip on a discount airline. Today, saving has
become such a habit for me that I hardly ever think about it.
Once you've learned how to do it, you never forget or want to
stop. Your savings habit gives you a good feeling of security,
freedom and self-confidence.

Why not do the same for yourself? How much would you
like to save this year? Decide the amount, and then go for it.
And plan on rewarding yourself with a night out with friends or
a new outfit if, and only if, you hit your target. The better you
get at creating ingenious little plans for increasing the size of
your savings cushion, the sooner you will reach your target,
and your treat.

It's very important that you change your perception of the
money you put into a savings account. It's not about depriving

yourself. Instead, the money you save is a gift that you are giving for yourself: the gift of independence. If a life crisis should happen to you, you won't have to go cap in hand to your family or hope for a government handout. The money you have saved will give you some control, some breathing room to think and plan. As well as insulation from life's nasty surprises, saving affords you physical and mental freedom. Once you start seeing it in this way, you'll find it's not so hard to save after all.

Deciding Where to Save

Your emergency nest egg should be completely *liquid*. In other words, it should be accessible immediately and at full value in case of an emergency. If you are building your lifeboat fund together with your spouse or partner, make sure it is accessible to both of you, so that if one is incapacitated and can't get to the account, the other one can. The easiest way to do this is by opening a joint account. Of course, this assumes a level of trust between you, since either owner of a joint account has full access to the money. If you are uncomfortable with opening a joint account, then don't do it. You can save separately.

Select a local bank or building society account that offers the highest rate of interest. You'll find interest rate comparisons in the weekend newspapers or on the internet. *Base rates* in the UK are set by the Bank of England, and most banks and building societies will offer rates on savings accounts within a few percentage points of the base rate. Typically, the rate increases when the base rate is raised and decreases when it is lowered. This is known as a *variable rate*. A few banks and building societies offer *fixed rates* on savings accounts, but this is less common. The interest rates paid on deposits in these accounts do not change for a specified period.

Some accounts require 30, 60 or 90 days' notice before you can make a withdrawal. Choose such an account only if it pays a substantially higher rate of interest. In a crisis, you can still withdraw your money immediately, but you will forfeit the equivalent of 30, 60 or 90 days' interest.

Many building societies offer *tiered rates* for savings accounts. This system pays a higher interest rate as your savings balance increases. In short, the more you save, the more you are rewarded. This system gives you a clear incentive to try to increase your account balance in order to enjoy a higher interest rate.

Some savings accounts provide cards offering instant access to your money, with others you can withdraw cash by going to the branch in person. Postal accounts also offer good interest rates, but you can only make deposits or withdrawals by post, so it could take several days before funds are credited to your savings account.

It's a terrific idea to help a child catch the savings habit with his or her own account. The government now offers to help you start saving or investing for your child through the Child

Trust Fund. It gives £250 to every child born after 1 September 2002. Children born into a family with a low income receive an additional £250. The Child Trust Fund (CTF) provides clear information that helps a family choose the saving or investment product that they feel is most appropriate to their long-term goals and risk tolerance. More information about the CTF can be obtained from the website www.childtrust-fund.gov.uk or by calling 0845 302 1470.

Some banks also offer children's savings accounts that may pay better interest rates than adult accounts. Some even offer goodies like magazines, stickers, piggy banks, club memberships and the opportunity to compete for prizes like tickets to film premières, family holidays or the latest PlayStation game.

Tax-advantaged Saving

If you are a taxpayer, the interest you receive on bank and building society accounts is subject to tax. The tax will be deducted by the bank at a rate of 20%. If you are a basic-rate taxpayer, that's all you will pay (even though the basic rate is currently higher than this). However, if you are a higher-rate taxpayer (currently 40%), you'll have to make up the difference when you file your self-assessment tax return. All interest on bank and building society accounts must be listed in your tax return.

If you're not a taxpayer, you will have to sign a form asking the bank or building society not to deduct tax at source. Parents can do this on behalf of their children. If you are a 10% taxpayer, let the building society deduct 20%, then claim it back by filling in a form called R40. In essence you are using the government to help you save.

Fortunately, there are ways to minimise the tax bite on your savings. One of the best and most popular is the *individual savings account*, or ISA.

ISAs were introduced by the government in 1999 to replace TESSAs (tax-exempt special savings accounts) and PEPs (personal equity plans).

The great benefit of an ISA is that ayou do not have to pay any further tax on the gains made on money invested in them. In reality an ISA is an account in which you can save money as cash, invest it in stocks and shares, or both, depending on the type of ISA account you open – either a maxi ISA or a mini ISA. You can open an ISA through a bank, a building society, a financial adviser, a broker or through an online fund supermarket. However, not all types are sold by each kind of adviser. For more specific details and clear, up-to-date information about ISAs, current contribution limits, providers and the types of ISAs they offer (cash, stocks and shares, or both), I suggest that you visit the Her Majesty's Revenue and Customs website, which has a section dedicated to ISAs (www.hmrc.gov.uk/isa).

For your lifeboat fund, consider opening a mini cash ISA. It's secure and liquid enough for emergency purposes. It offers instant access and a variable rate of interest that is usually higher than that offered by a straightforward deposit account. Mini cash ISAs don't appear to be advertised as much as stocks and shares ISAs; however, they are widely available.

There are some restrictions on ISAs that you should keep in mind (see the HMRC website):

- There may be fees for setting up or making withdrawals from an ISA.
- You can only register an ISA in a single name, so your partner won't be able to access it.
- If you open a mini ISA, you can't open a maxi ISA in the same year. The reverse is also true.
- Once you have paid in the maximum allowed, you cannot top up the account again after you have made a withdrawal.

If you are a taxpayer, it makes total sense to use your ISA allowance in some way every year. You may as well save on your taxes if you can!

Another way to save on taxes is through National Savings & Investments (NS&I). This scheme was set up in 1861 to persuade British workers to save, and it currently has more than thirty million customers. There are various tax-free savings options available through NS&I, including mini cash ISAs, *fixed-interest savings certificates* (from £100 up to £15,000) and *index-linked savings certificates* (also from £100 up to

£15,000). If you buy a savings certificate, your money will be locked away for a fixed period of two to five years. A fixed-interest savings certificate pays a predetermined interest rate, while an index-linked savings certificate pays a variable rate that is guaranteed to beat inflation.

NS&I also offers *Premium Bonds*, which combine the opportunity to save with the appeal of gambling. When you buy a Premium Bond in an amount from £100 to £30,000, the interest earned goes to buy chances of winning cash prizes in a government-sponsored lottery, with prizes ranging from £50 to a £1 million jackpot. Any prize you win is tax-free. Of course, most people who buy Premium Bonds don't win large prizes, but they do get back the money they laid out in the first place, which is more than you can say with an ordinary lottery.

You'll find leaflets describing all these government-sponsored savings products in your local post office. You can buy them over the counter, by phone on 0845 964 5000 or online at www.nsandi.com.

What Next?

Once your lifeboat account is in place, your life is likely to change for the better. Firstly, your stress level will go down. Even if you weren't consciously worrying before, money fears can worm their way into your mind. Once you have a savings account with three to six months' take-home pay in it, you'll be able to sleep at night, knowing that you and your family have some protection against all but the most horrific of personal and financial emergencies. Keep in mind that three to six months' take-home pay is a prudent but not a generous amount. If a larger lifeboat account would make you more comfortable – one year's take-home pay, for example – then save that amount. For me, the more I have, the less I worry about the unexpected.

Better still, you're now in a position to launch a more ambitious programme of saving and investing – one that can help you go beyond protecting the good things you already have to enjoy a whole world of new benefits. I'll show you how to get started in the next chapter.

2 | INVESTMENT GOALS AND RISKS

Defining Your Goals

Once you've eliminated your consumer debt and built up your lifeboat account, you're in a position to begin saving and investing with your personal dreams and goals in mind.

Take some time to think about where you would like to be five years from now. Then ten years from now. And then at retirement age. Where do you want to live? How would you like to spend your leisure time? What ambitions do you want to fulfil? Would you like to buy a second home by the sea? To take six months or a year off work and travel round the world? To convert your attic into a loft or studio? Is your primary goal to see your children well educated and successfully launched into the world? Perhaps you'd like to donate money to a charity close to your heart, or start a trust fund to benefit your grandchildren?

Any or all of these dreams may be realised with the help of a plan for saving and investing. Here's how to create such a plan. On a sheet of paper, write the heading 'Saving Goals'. On this paper, list one to three short-term goals (goals you hope to achieve within the next three to five years), then one to three longer-term goals (which will take longer than five years to achieve). Think about when you would like to achieve each goal, and note the number of months between now and that date. (See the sample form on page 22.) Of course, if your have a spouse or partner, the two of you should do this exercise together.

Next, put a price on your dreams in pounds and pence. Estimate the amount you will need to achieve these goals. Be as accurate as you can. This may require a bit of research. Is buying a second home one of your long-term goals? Remember that in addition to the deposit required to buy the house, there will most likely be the extra costs of renovating, landscaping, painting and furnishing. Are you saving for a dream wedding? Include all the costs, from frocks and flowers to a fabulous honeymoon. It is important to know what you expect each of your dreams to cost so that you will know the financial goals you are working towards.

Divide the total cost of each dream or goal by the number of months between now and when you want to realise it. The answer tells you how much you will need to save per month. For example, the first goal listed in the sample form below is a

Saving Goals Sample Form

GOAL	COST	TARGET DATE	COST/MONTH
Wedding	£12,000	12 months	£1,000.00
Loft conversion	£10,000	36 months	£277.78
Pay off mortgage	£30,000	120 months	£250.00
University fees	£18,000	180 months	£100.00
TOTAL			£1,627.78

wedding to take place 12 months in the future. Dividing the total cost of £12,000 by the number of months gives £1,000, which is the amount that must be saved per month. (Yes, for the purposes of this exercise, I am *ignoring* interest and other ways money can grow. To include those in the table would make the maths rather complicated. You should be able to achieve your saving goals somewhat more quickly than indicated if interest earned on your money is taken into consideration.)

Once you've listed all your most important goals and calculated what it will cost to achieve them, consider the monthly total. After you pay each month's bills and essential expenses, can you manage to save the full amount required? If so, fantastic – get started today! If not, you'll need to make some adjustments.

One approach is to prioritise your goals. In the example above, if you can't find £1,627.78 a month to save, you might choose to concentrate on saving for the wedding for the first year. You can start saving for the other three goals after the vows have been said. (Of course, eliminating 12 months from your savings plan for those other goals will require you to increase the monthly amount you save for them, if you still want to reach them within the same amount of time.)

You might also want to consider whether you can increase your income to make your dreams more affordable. Can you do some overtime work, take on a second job, or start a small business out of your home in your spare time? If you devote all of the income from your other jobs to your savings plan, you may be able to achieve goals that would otherwise remain out of reach.

An alternative approach is to allow more time to reach some goals. Doing this exercise can be the reality check we need to realise that very few of us earn enough to make all our dreams achieveable overnight.

From Saving to Investing

You can also improve your chances of reaching your goals – especially your long-term goals – by moving beyond saving to investing.

Remember our definitions from the previous chapter: saving means putting aside money in a risk-free account, while investing means taking on an amount of risk in order to achieve faster growth for your money. Once you've eliminated your consumer debt, built up your lifeboat account, and covered your insurance needs, you can think about investing the money you are setting aside for your life goals. This is money with which you can afford to take (modest) chances, since it's not the money you will need to rely on in case of an emergency. However, it is essential to be aware of your own risk tolerance. If you are uncomfortable with investing, think it is too risky for you, or don't want your money to be at risk in any way, then don't invest. Stick with keeping your money in a high-interest account at a building society or bank.

Investing can yield greater returns than saving, but it is also more complicated. There are many different types of investments, each with its particular advantages and disadvantages. Choosing the right investments for yourself depends on many factors, including the nature of your goals, the time frame within which you hope to reach those goals, your personality and comfort level with taking risks with your money.

In the next few pages, I'll offer some basic guidance about how to begin thinking about your investment choices. And in later chapters, we'll delve in more detail into the specifics about how individual investments work.

Let's start by considering the three broad categories of investment products that most people ought to consider:

- A *share* represents part-ownership in a company. When you buy shares, you are entitled to receive dividends, which is a portion of the profits (if any) made by the company. All dividends must be declared by the board of directors of a company. Dividends are typically declared and paid semiannually. In addition, if the company's turnover and profits grow, the market price of its shares will also increase, rising higher than the price you paid for them. Thus you would be able to sell them for a profit, called capital gains. Of course, there are no guarantees that the shares of any company will increase in value. If the company's growth prospects decline, so will the value of the shares you own. Such an event could result in a loss.

- A *bond* is essentially an IOU. When you buy a bond, you are lending money to a company or a government agency, which in turn promises to pay you a fixed amount of interest (called the *coupon rate*) at regular intervals (usually semiannually or annually) until the bond matures. At maturity, the company or government repays the principal (typically £100). Bonds issued by private companies are *corporate bonds*; those issued by the UK government are *government bonds* or *gilts*. High-grade corporate bonds and government securities usually appeal to conservative investors because of the reliability of their interest payments.

- A *pooled investment* is a fund of customers' monies that is invested in a diversified collection (or *portfolio*) of securities (stock and/or bonds). The portfolio is managed by an investment professional who decides what securities to buy into and sell out of the portfolio. When you buy into a pooled investment (such as a unit trust or an investment trust), you are purchasing part-ownership in that portfolio, and you are entitled to a percentage of the dividends (on stocks), interest (on bonds) and capital gains (or losses) earned by the portfolio as a whole. Not all pooled fund portfolios are managed by an investment professional. Some portfolios consist of the shares that make up a specific stock index, like the FTSE 250. These funds, called *tracker funds*, are designed to move in tandem with a specific index as well as provide the exact dividend return and capital appreciation of the index they are based on. The shares in the portfolio change only when the companies included in the index change; therefore there is no need for an investment manager to choose stocks. As a result, tracker funds have lower overall expenses than managed funds.

Within these three broad categories, there are many different types of shares, bonds and unit trusts. Each has its own characteristics that make it appropriate for a particular type of investor or investment strategy. And of course there are other, more specialised types of investments that don't fit into these three categories – most are those the average investor should avoid, as I'll explain later.

The Risk Pyramid

VERY RISKY

Options, futures, and other derivatives
antiques, art, coins, stamps, collectibles
High-risk shares: Penny shares, small-cap shares
High-risk bonds: junk or corporate bonds

SOMEWHAT RISKY

Blue-chip shares, mid-cap shares
Unit trust, OEIC, tracker funds

LESS RISKY

High-grade corporate bonds
Bond funds

VIRTUALLY RISK-FREE

Gilts
National savings
Banks and building societies

Understanding Your Risk Tolerance

As I've stated, every investment carries with it some degree of
risk. But the level and kind of risk varies greatly from one
investment type to another. One useful way of thinking about

investments is the Risk Pyramid (shown on the previous page). It lists many well-known investment vehicles, arranged in order from those with the least risk at the bottom (where the pyramid is more stable) to those with the greatest risk at the top. (You may not recognise the names of every investment category listed. Not to worry: they'll be explained later in this book.)

You may notice that, broadly speaking, shares tend to fall at the higher-risk end of the risk pyramid, while investment or pooled funds and bonds are lower risk. More risky investments are more *volatile* – that is, their prices rise and fall more severely and less predictably. Perhaps you wonder, why would any investor choose a more risky investment when safer choices are available? The reason is simple: as a general rule, the more risk you take, the greater your potential gains; the less risk you take, the smaller your gains are likely to be.

Smart investing, then, is about balancing the hope of gains against the risk of loss. But how do you go about achieving the proper balance for yourself? How do you maximise your potential profit while minimising the risk of losing money? Much of the rest of this book will focus on these vital skills.

Kinds of Investment Risk

To begin, it's important to understand what *investment risk* really means. Otherwise, you'll have little hope of making informed decisions about what kinds of risk you're willing to accept, as well as those you want to avoid. So let's start by taking a look at the different kinds of investment risk. Then I'll show you ways in which you can manage or lessen (but not eliminate) these kinds of risk when choosing an investment.

Here are the most important forms of investment risk:

- *Company-specific risk*, also called *stock-specific risk* and *unsystematic risk*, is the risk that shares in a specific company will plummet due to a decline in turnover, poor management, an ill-advised expansion, failure of a new product or the emergence of a stronger competitor. If this happens to a company in which you've invested, then you will lose money as the value of the shares drops. You could even lose the total amount you've invested if the company goes bust.

- *Sector risk* is the risk that share values in a particular industry, such as airlines, biotechnology or consumer goods, will decline because of trends in that industry or a downturn in the economy. For example, the travel industry has suffered in recent years as a result of 9/11, the threat of terrorism and the sluggish economy (which discourages business travellers). Consequently, investors who held shares of hotel companies, airlines, cruise lines and other travel businesses experienced poor returns on the money invested. Similarly, high-technology shares collapsed in 2000 when rosy predictions about the 'new economy' created by the Internet began to seem exaggerated. Sectors can, and often do, rebound from such declines, but it may take some time. If your money is overly concentrated in just one industry and there's a downturn, sector risk may cost you dearly.

- *Market or systemic risk* is the risk that the entire investment market may decline in value. When this happens, investors describe the decline as a *bear market*. (The opposite, when market values generally increase, is called a *bull market*.) Both bear-market and bull-market cycles come and go, but while they last they can have a serious impact on investors. If, for example, you need to sell your investments during a bear market, you may lose money.

- *Inflation risk* is the risk that the money you invest will lose some of its purchasing power due to price inflation in the economy – that is, an increase in the cost of buying goods and services. For example, suppose you invest in a bond that pays 5% interest. If inflation increases so that the price of things you buy to meet your basic needs increases by an average of 8% per year, then the money you've invested in the bond is growing more slowly than overall prices. As a result, the goods and services you can buy with the money you've invested and the income it generates shrinks. In short, your money buys less, which means it is decreasing in value.

- *Currency risk* is the risk that a change in the value of a foreign currency may reduce the value of an investment that is denominated in a different currency. For example, suppose you invest in a US company. If the value of the dollar declines in relation to the pound, then the value of the money (dividends) you receive from the investment is worth less to you. If the value of the dollar increases relative to the pound, then the money paid in US dollars is much more attractive. Another example would be a UK company that does lots of business in the US. If the US dollar declines, there could be a drop in turnover and profits when they are exchanged into sterling. On the other hand, if the dollar increases in value, the company may experience an increase in turnover and profits, not based in increased business, but based solely on exchange-rate fluctuations.

- *Political risk* is the risk that an investment in a specific country, geographical region or a business that is heavily dependent on a country or region might fall in value or become totally worthless if there were a sudden change of government or political unrest. This problem is most acute in many of the emerging or developing markets. A sudden change in government could lead to tighter restrictions on businesses, hurting the the country's or region's expected economic growth. In a worst-case scenario, businesses may be suddenly nationalised by a new government, making all securities owed by individual investors worthless.

Does all of this talk about risk make you feel nervous? That's understandable. The complexity of investment risk is one of the big reasons that even seasoned professionals sometimes lose money when they invest. Fortunately, over the long term, most investment markets tend to rise in value rather than fall, although there can be a long period of decline, a bear market. This is because – again, in the long run – the economies of the UK and the world tend to expand and grow rather than shrink. Populations grow, companies sell more products, technologies advance, new industries are launched, and incomes rise, all of which can generate growing profits for investors.

So, over time, if you select the right companies or business sectors, you should benefit by seeing the value of your money grow faster than it would in a traditional savings account. The trick or talent is to find those industries or sectors that you can develop a good knowledge of and that will provide the growth you desire without you having to take on excessive risk. You will need to give the investment a reasonable period of time to reach your expected goals. Expect the occasional bumps in the road, and do not expect to be right 100% of the time. The key is to be right more often than you are wrong.

Rules for Managing Risk

Some people would like to be able to invest without taking on any risk at all. This is not possible. For those who can't bear the idea of even modest risk, they should save their money in strictly risk-free vehicles like bank, building society or National Savings accounts. As we've seen, any money you put into these accounts is not subject to loss due to volatility. The problem is that because these accounts are safe, the interest earned on them can be small. Your money grows slowly. If, however, inflation increases and the cost of goods goes up, the actual purchasing power of your totally safe money will decline. If you have ambitious financial goals, risk-free saving will probably be inadequate to achieve them. Unless you are disciplined and aggressive, it will be necessary to take on some risk in pursuit of faster capital growth. But how do you decide how much risk to take? Here are some guidelines that successful investors use.

- *Put short-term money into low-risk investments; put long-term money into higher-risk investments.* For example, money you plan to use as a deposit on property or to pay for a wedding next year should be put into a risk-free savings account or low-risk investments, like gilts or high-grade corporate bonds. Your return will be low, but you will have the comfort of knowing that your money is not likely to lose value. In contrast, money you are setting aside to pay for your children's university fees in 10 to 15 years can be invested in higher-growth, higher-risk investments, such as an actively managed unit trust, a tracker fund (explained more in the next chapter) or a collection of individual blue-chip shares. When you are investing over such a long period of time, you can endure the inevitable ups and downs of stocks, bonds and unit trusts, realising that over the long term the stock market has historically tended to outperform other types of investment.

- *The younger you are, the more risk you can afford to take.* In this case I am referring to any money that you are putting away for the long term, like your pension. Because the time horizon for these goals is so far away, young people can be more aggressive with their investment money, if it is appropriate for their risk tolerance. The longer time horizon means that when the inevitable market downturn occurs, young people can be patient, riding it out and reaping potentially greater financial rewards when the bull market returns.

- *Don't take unnecessary risks with money you can't afford to lose.* Be careful to distinguish between money that you are investing for important goals like a second home or retirement and 'fun money' with which you can take some chances. Think of your savings as falling into three categories: 1) money whose loss would seriously affect your well-being, 2) money that you set aside for long-term goals that you may or may not want to put at risk and 3) 'extra' money that you would hate to lose but could live without. Money in the first category belongs in risk-free vehicles. Money in the second category can be placed in low-or moderate-risk investments. And if you have any money in the third category, which many people don't, you can use it to invest in higher-risk securities, like those in the emerging areas such as biotech. This does not mean you should be reckless with this money. Make sure you are emotionally prepared in advance to lose the money. And if you make an investment that proves profitable, don't suddenly begin thinking you are an investment genius. Consider yourself very lucky and put the profits into a less risky investment or a savings account.

- *The more experienced and knowledgeable you are, the greater the risks you may be comfortable taking.* As a novice investor, you should begin with low-risk investments until you develop an understanding of how specific types of investment products and the overall market work. You may want to test yourself by 'paper investing' before putting your money into the market. Later, as your understanding of both the markets and your own risk tolerance improves, then you may want to try selecting the actual shares and bonds yourself. If you do this, it is always important to remain a bit sceptical of the market and restrained in your estimation of your investment abilities.

- *Pay attention to the voice inside you.* Everyone has a different level of risk tolerance, based on their personality, upbringing, values and fears. The investments you choose should be ones you feel comfortable with on an intellectual and gut level. The legendary American financier J. P. Morgan was once approached by a man who had invested a large sum of money and made good gains. He was happy about the profits, he explained, but he was having trouble sleeping at night for

worrying about his portfolio. J. P. Morgan's advice was
succinct and wise: 'Sell down to sleeping point.'

If you're not sure what level of risk you ought to accept, err on
the side of caution. It's always easy to move some money
gradually into more risky (and potentially more lucrative)
investments. However, if you take too many risks too quickly,
it may take years not only to recoup the money you've lost, but
also to restore your confidence that any type of investing is
worthwhile.

Asset Allocation

Whether this is your first time investing or you already have
some experience, here's an important principal to keep in
mind: do not put all of your eggs in one basket. This familiar
warning holds true no matter how much money you have to
invest.

If you have only a small amount to begin with, it is probably
best that you limit your investment choices to a diversified
investment or pooled fund with a long history of delivering
good, relatively steady returns. Buying into a pooled fund gives
you 1) access to the skills of an investment professional who
selects the securities in which the fund is invested and 2)
immediate diversification because there are usually shares of a

wide range of different companies held in the unit trust's underlying portfolio.

If you have enough money to buy individual shares, you should strategically aim to create a portfolio that includes different asset classes and different business sectors within each asset class. You are thus creating your own diversified portfolio.

Think of diversification as an important risk-management strategy. The underlying principle is simple. When you buy the shares and/or bonds of companies in different business sectors, the overall risk of loss is reduced. If, for example, you invest in shares of 20 different companies, you'll only lose a small amount of the total value of your investment if one of the companies goes bankrupt. In contrast, if all your money is invested in a single company's shares or bonds, the risk of loss is greater. Should that one company fall on hard times or be forced into insolvency, all of the money you have invested may be lost.

Deciding exactly how to diversify your investment portfolio is known as *asset allocation*, and there are many ways to approach it using both individual securities (stock and bonds) and different types of pooled investments. It will take time and thought for you to find the one that suits you best. Below are some examples of different combinations – represented in the form of pie charts – that may be suitable for investors with different investment objectives and risk tolerances.

In each chart, three asset classes are shown. 'Cash' refers to risk-free savings in a bank or building society. (This can also be held in a mini cash ISA.) 'Bonds' and 'shares' were defined earlier in this chapter. Money invested in an investment fund can fall into either the bonds or shares asset class, depending on the investments in the trust's portfolio.

Please note that I am not making any specific recommendations regarding the right asset allocation for you. These are illustrations only, which will provide you with some guidelines. The final choice of percentages is yours, always keeping in mind your own risk tolerance. Basic measures for determining percentages are age, preservation of capital, need for current income and whether your approach will be conservative or aggressive.

A. *The Age-adjusted Mix*
An asset-allocation model that many people like and find easy to follow is the Age-adjusted Mix. Its formula is designed to change your investment mix from focusing on capital appreciation in your early years to a more conservative approach whose objective is preservation of capital as you grow older. The formula is:

$$\frac{100\% - \text{Your age}}{= \text{Percentage of assets invested in shares or unit trusts}}$$

The remaining percentage would be invested in bonds (or a mixture of bonds and risk-free cash). Thus, when you are 30 years old, this mix would allocate 70% of your investment money to stocks and 30% to bonds or investment funds that invest in bonds. When you are 50, you would have 50% in stocks and 50% in high-grade bonds. You would adjust the percentage each year, typically on your birthday or at the beginning of the year. Rebalancing the percentages once a year enables the investor to capture some of the capital gains made on shares and invest that money in more conservative bonds in which he or she would earn interest.

B. *The Income Mix (25% cash, 35% bonds, 40% shares)*

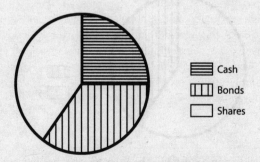

Cash

Bonds

Shares

This formula may suit someone in their fifties to sixties who wants to invest for current income as well as growth. The shares should be in large, well-established companies (called blue-chip companies) rather than new start-ups. Such shares have a greater likelihood of providing a more reliable stream of dividend income, and the shares are less likely to be extremely volatile – i.e. move up and down in price by large amounts over time. While this asset allocation may not provide the type of gains to brag about at a garden party, you could take some comfort in the fact that preservation of capital is also one of the objectives of this allocation.

C. The Conservative or Balanced Mix (40% Bonds, 60% Shares)

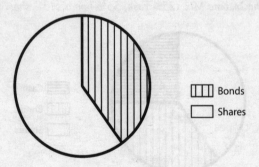

This allocation model, like the previous one, has preservation of capital as one of its goals. It seeks to provide steady income (from the interest paid on the bonds) while offering some opportunity for capital appreciation depending on the types of stocks or unit trusts that complete the remainder of the portfolio. It is important to rebalance this allocation annually. If shares have grown more in value, you sell them and invest the capital gains in lower-risk bonds. If bonds have outperformed stocks, then you sell off some of the bonds and use the profits to buy shares that may be temporarily undervalued and are getting ready to rise in price. With this allocation, one is unlikely to be either the biggest winner or, perhaps most importantly, the biggest loser.

D. *The Moderately Aggressive Mix (10% cash, 35% bonds, 55% shares)*

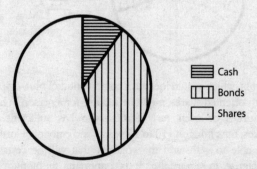

≡ Cash

▥ Bonds

▢ Shares

This is a moderate-to-conservative asset-allocation mix that might suit an investor in his or her forties whose investment objectives could be met with a mixture of short-term and retirement goals. The cash fund can be used to buy more shares or bonds whenever either category of investment looks attractive, so the actual proportion of shares can vary between 55% and 65%.

E. *The Aggressive Mix (15% cash, 15% bonds, 70% shares)*

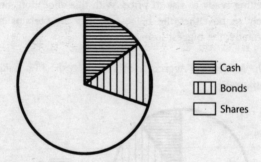

- Cash
- Bonds
- Shares

This mix, which would include a combination of blue-chip and growth-oriented shares, might be suitable for a person in his or her thirties or even early forties who has sufficient cash reserves, time horizon (10 to 15 years) and emotional fortitude to be able to withstand the volatility that will be certain to characterise this portfolio. It is important to monitor this portfolio regularly and to have established in advance the point when you will sell a losing position in order to cut your losses. Keep in mind that if all of the shares are in high-risk industries, then this would be a very aggressive asset allocation.

F. *The Very Aggressive Mix (5% cash, 10% bonds, 85% shares)*

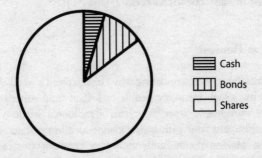

Cash
Bonds
Shares

This is a fairly high-risk portfolio with the potential to produce high returns over the long term and substantial losses if there is a sudden market downturn or a prolonged bear market. It is suitable for a young, risk-tolerant investor interested in capital appreciation over the long term and prepared to accept losses if they occur. An investor with this allocation mix must be prepared to take a long-term view of his or her investments, be able to accept short-term price volatility and be committed to monitoring the investments at regular intervals in order to determine a good time to capture profits and cut losses. This type of portfolio is not suitable for most people.

Deciding on an asset-allocation model or strategy only gives you the broad outline of your investment plan. It doesn't tell you how to choose the specific share, bond or unit trust that will fit into each slice of your pie. Be patient – I'll explain how to do that in subsequent chapters.

Safe as Houses?

You may have been wondering why I haven't said a word about property, which for many people in Britain (and America) is the most valuable asset they have. Traditional wisdom has viewed buying your primary residence as a form of enforced saving. Making the monthly mortgage payment (instead of paying rent) was thought to be like putting money in a bank account. Because most property prices have gone up over the long run, any money put into property could be expected to grow at a decent, and sometimes impressive rate, while having substantially less risk than that associated with investing in shares. I believe this basic wisdom holds true for most people and that buying property is a relatively safe, although hardly certain, way to increase one's net worth over time. And keep in mind that old adage 'Location, location, location' when buying the house in which you will live. If, however, you are buying to let or buying property to refurbish and quickly resell, other factors must be considered.

Owning property for investment offers both potential gains and the risk of loss. The risks inherent in property vary widely; in fact, they are different in every single area of the country. This makes it hard to formulate a property-based investment strategy for the average person to follow.

As a very general rule, property prices tend to rise over time. But the boom-and-bust cycles (like the ones we saw in the late 1970s and early 1990s) illustrate the dangers. Just ask anyone who ended up with negative equity or who was forced to sell their investment property at a loss during these times. The reality is that you may not be able to sell your home at the price you want at the time you need the money. On the other hand, at the time you sell and can get the price you want, you may find that other house prices have risen as well. Some sellers have found that moving to a smaller place is likely to cost them more. And let's not forget about the many costs involved in buying and selling property – the surveyors' and solicitors' fees, stamp duty, the estate agent's commission and removal costs. These will further reduce the profit potential of a property investment.

As I write this, I am reminded of many of the bad property-investment stories (perhaps they are better called confessions) I have been told but no one wants to believe: a young man who bought too much property on too much credit and could not afford to make all of the mortgage payments when interest rates started to rise; a young lady who overestimated the speed of renting and the amount of rent on a buy-to-let flat and ended up losing money each month until she was able to sell the flat nearly a year after she bought it; and a friend who bought a property in the City during the 1990s property boom and was in negative equity for nearly five years before he was able to sell the flat at exactly what he paid for it, having lost money on all of the maintenance costs incurred over that time. If you want to buy property as an investment, be aware that there are a number of things that can go wrong – and at some point probably will go wrong. Do your calculations carefully, dispassionately, and realistically. And be prepared to accept the fact that buying property is never risk-free. We will look at property as investment in more detail in Chapter 7.

The Opportunity Is in the Details

So far I've provided you with an overview of the investment landscape. Now it's time to focus on specific details. Over the next few chapters, I'll discuss the factors you need to consider before you make a specific investment in order to make sure that the choice is suitable for you, both in terms of your investment objectives and your risk tolerance.

3 | INVESTING IN POOLED FUNDS

Dipping Your Toe in the Investment Waters

Practice may not make perfect, but it surely helps. That's why, for many novices, investing in a *unit trust*, *OIEC* or *investment trust* is an excellent first step into the world of investing.

A unit trust is a large portfolio of shares, bonds or both selected by a knowledgeable, experienced fund manager. Pooling money from thousands of individual investors, the manager buys shares and bonds he or she believes are poised to rise in value, sells those that seem ready to falter and looks for opportunities to profit from company growth and the payment of dividends. When the overall value of the portfolio increases, so does the value of the units owned by individual investors. Of course, the reverse can also happen: the value of your investment may fall, particularly during a bear market, when market values in general are declining.

An *open-ended investment company* (OEIC) is another type of fund that closely resembles a unit trust. Like a unit trust it is an investment company that uses a pool of investors' money to buy and sell securities in accordance with a stated investment objective. OEIC shares are bought and sold at a specific price, the *net asset value* (NAV), which is based on the closing prices of the securities in the portfolio at the end of each day's trading. A sales charge may be added to the NAV when you buy them. For technical reasons, OEICs are simpler to market overseas than unit trusts, and they are widely popular in the US, where they're known as *mutual funds*.

An *investment trust* works in a similar way to a unit trust, but with some key differences. Investment trust shares are listed on a stock exchange and can trade at a market price below their NAV (known as a discount) or above their NAV (called a premium) depending on demand. Another important difference is that investment trusts can borrow against their total value to buy additional investments. This is called gearing and can make them significantly more risky than unit trusts. An advantage of investment trusts is that costs and changes tend to be low and, if the investments bought using borrowed money appreciate, the returns will be greater.

Investing in a pooled fund, then, is like having a savvy investment manager working on your behalf. Of course, there's no guarantee that the result will be stellar; as we noted in Chapter 2, even skilled investment professionals sometimes lose money. Keep in mind, though, that fund managers have every incentive to make wise decisions on behalf of their investors. Another advantage is instant diversification.

As we explained in Chapter 2, diversification is a key principle of risk reduction. When you put all your eggs in one basket (i.e. one investment), the danger of losing your money if something goes wrong is much greater. By contrast, when your portfolio contains a range of varied investments, it's unlikely that any single economic event or business trend will devastate all of the securities in the portfolio.

Thus, such forms of investment risk as sector risk and company-specific risk can be greatly reduced when a portfolio is properly diversified. Studies have shown that a portfolio should contain shares in at least a dozen different companies in different business sectors to enjoy the benefits of diversification.

Unfortunately, diversification can be difficult for an individual investor to achieve. Because of transaction costs and brokerage firms' policies about minimum investment amounts, it's not practical to buy very small quantities of company shares. Therefore, an investor with just a few hundred or a few thousand pounds to invest would probably be unable to purchase shares in more than one or two companies – not enough to achieve real diversification.

This is where a pooled fund has an advantage. A typical fund will hold shares in more than twenty companies, and its manager will avoid putting more than 5% of the fund's total assets into shares of any one company. So when you invest in the fund, you've instantly achieved diversification.

Types of Funds

In recent years, as millions of people have been attracted to the advantages of pooled funds, the number of funds has grown enormously, including specialised funds designed to meet the investment objectives of specific groups of investors. As you'll see, different types of funds have different risk characteristics. Some, like those that invest in high-grade bonds and blue-chip stocks, can be low risk, while others, like those whose objective is aggressive growth, will be more risky. This additional risk is reflected in a fund's price volatility.

Here's a quick description of some of the most popular types of funds available today:

- *Equity-income funds* invest in shares of companies that pay high dividends – that is, they distribute a large portion of the profits they earn to their shareholders. An equity-income fund is usually considered to be conservative and therefore may be appropriate for investors whose objective is to create a stream of income from their investments that they will be able to live on.
- *Capital-growth funds* invest in the shares of small- or medium-

sized companies whose turnover and profits are expected to grow rapidly in the years to come. These types of companies pay little if any dividends; instead, they reinvest their profits in the business to help it expand. Investors make money on the increase of the price of the companies' shares held in the portfolio. Capital-growth funds can be very volatile, depending on the specific companies or business sectors in which the fund's assets are invested.

- *Small-cap funds* specialise in shares of young, unproven companies often in new or emerging business areas. The name is short for 'small capitalisation', which refers to the total market value of such companies' ordinary shares outstanding in the market. A small-cap fund is likely to be volatile and high risk: in a bad year, you could lose a substantial portion of your investment; and in a good year, you would have huge capital gains. These funds are definitely not for conservative, low-risk investors.

- *Global funds* invest in shares of companies around the world (including some within the UK). Because the economies of the emerging or developing markets in such places as Asia and the former Iron Curtain countries are often expanding at a much faster rate than the older, established economies of Western Europe and North America, the growth potential of companies in these markets can produce a substantial investment return. It is important that the portfolio manager has an understanding of and experience in these markets in order to make the best investment decisions. Don't expect a smooth ride to big profits. Brace yourself for some big price swings along the way, as these countries are subject to unpredictable political, economic and financial crises.

- *International funds* invest only outside the UK and can sometimes be riskier than global funds, depending on the international companies the portfolio manager selects. Currency or foreign-exchange risk is usually a significant factor in the return you can expect for this type of fund.

- *Sector funds* invest in companies within particular industries, such as pharmaceuticals, food, entertainment and media, financial services, technology and transportation. If you believe that a business sector is due for significant growth because of economic, cultural or social trends, you might want to consider investing in a sector fund devoted to it.

- *Ethical funds* invest in companies that meet particular moral or social criteria. For example, an ethical fund may avoid companies that manufacture tobacco products or military equipment, or it may invest in companies known for their progressive employment and environmental practices. Some ethical funds have impressive returns over time, so it's certainly possible to 'do well' at the same time as you 'do good' with your investments.

- *Bond funds* invest in bonds – corporate bonds and/or UK-government bonds – rather than shares. These funds produce interest income and capital gains if the bonds appreciate in value. The most significant risk is interest-rate risk. If interest rates rise, bond prices will fall and you may experience a loss on your investment. We'll describe how they work in Chapter 5.

Of course, an individual's investment portfolio should include more than one type of unit trust or fund. For example, suppose you want to build a portfolio using the 'Conservative or Balanced Mix' (described on page 40), which consists of 40% bonds and 60% shares. You could use 40% of your money to buy one or more bond funds. With the remaining 60%, you might choose a mixture of share funds so as to achieve a comfortable blend of conservative and capital-growth-oriented investments. For example, you could allocate half of this money to an equity-income fund and the other half to a capital-growth fund. (It's a bit like blending coffees – there are so many flavours available that almost anyone can put together a combination that will suit his or her taste.)

Funds with traditional and new investment objectives are being created all the time by financial services companies. You can find information about all existing unit trusts at the websites of the *Financial Times* (www.ft.com/fund) or the Financial Services Authority (www.fsa.gov.uk/tables).

Tracker Funds
One particular type of fund is important enough to deserve a

section of its own – the *tracker fund*. The portfolio of a tracker fund is designed to mirror (or 'track') the value of a well-known *stock-market index*, which is made up of specific companies chosen according to the index creator's criteria. Unlike the actively managed funds described in the last section, the shares that make up the portfolio of a particular tracker fund are not selected by a portfolio manager. In fact, these funds may have no active portfolio manager. The portfolio changes only as a result of a change in the companies whose shares make up the index. A tracker fund is therefore said to be unmanaged.

The best-known stock-market indexes in the UK were originally created by the *Financial Times* in partnership with the London Stock Exchange (LSE). Thus, they all have names that begin with 'FTSE' (pronounced 'footsie'), which stands for Financial Times Stock Exchange. The major indexes are explained below.

- *The FTSE 100 Index* consists of the UK's 100 largest blue-chip companies. It is the best-known UK stock-market index and is often called simply the FTSE.
- *The FTSE 250 Index* contains the 250 UK companies just below the giants of the FTSE 100 in size. It's often called the Mid-cap Index because it includes companies that are 'middle-sized' in terms of their total market value.
- *The FTSE Small-cap Index* includes around 350 smaller companies in the UK.

- *The FTSE All-share Index* combines the three indexes listed above – between 700 and 800 of the leading companies in the UK.

You've probably heard the names of some of these indexes on TV or the radio. Using a complex formula, the current share prices and number of outstanding shares of all the companies included in a particular index are used to determine the value of the index throughout the day and at the end of each day. Changes in the value of an index can interpreted in many ways, mostly to indicate the strength or weakness of the overall economy or business environment. Thus, when the FTSE 100 is up, investors feel that the prospects for big business and the overall economy are positive. If the FTSE 100 is down, investors may lack confidence in future business prospects, or they may be selling securities to capture any gains they have made.

When you invest in a tracker fund, your return, both from dividend income and capital gains (or losses), will be the same as or close to that produced by the index the tracker fund mimics. It is important to know that not every tracker fund has a portfolio that includes shares of all the companies on the index. Some funds choose, instead, to own a representative sampling. Nonetheless, the performance of a tracker fund will normally deviate from that of the index it is tracking by no more than a fraction of a per cent.

Now that you know what a tracker fund is and how it works, why would you consider investing in one? There are two good reasons. The first is lower fees. Because there is no management of the portfolio, management fees are minimal; therefore more of the investment returns end up in your pocket. The second reason is historical performance. A surprisingly large percentage of managed funds (usually a majority) underperformed the market as measured by the FTSE 100, for example; therefore choosing a tracker fund immediately gives you a better-than-average chance of getting a greater return than you would from most managed funds. This does not mean, however, that you cannot have losses. If you own an index fund during a bear market, then you will experience a loss on your investment just like everyone else as the market falls lower and lower. In fact, your losses may be worse than those of an actively managed fund where the portfolio manager can move the fund's investment money into risk-free cash.

Why is it so hard for fund managers to beat the indexes? The most common explanation is the *efficient market theory*, which is accepted by most scholars who have studied the stock market. According to the theory, all the available information about any company – good, bad or indifferent – is always fully reflected in the current price of its shares. This is because of the efficient ways this information is immediately disseminated to all participants in the markets via television, radio, the Internet, telephone or just plain gossip. Good news pushes the price up, and bad news causes the price to drop. Since all the news – real, anticipated or rumoured – plays a part in affecting the market, the price of any particular share at a given moment in time is correctly valued.

The only other things that can change the share price further are (1) new information that will become available in the future and 2) swings in investors' sentiment about the market. Both these factors are unknowable and unpredictable, which means that it is extremely unlikely that anyone can 'outsmart' the market consistently. Those who believe in the efficient market theory hold that the varying outcomes of different share investments – some very profitable, others not – are due mostly to luck.

But what about the superstar investors you've heard about – people like Warren Buffett and George Soros, who are famous for making millions through their shrewd market picks? Some of these superstars take advantage of *market inefficiencies* – periods of time when information is *not* equally available to all investors (and which are always short-lived). Others are, in fact, lucky, as shown by the years of lacklustre returns that often follow the years of success. Even Buffett and Soros have had bumpy periods in recent years.

The rationale for including tracker funds as part of your investment strategy or asset allocation is simple: since no one can beat the market consistently, why not give up trying and invest in the market as a whole? Tracker funds are an appropriate investment choice, especially for the novice investor or the person who simply doesn't want to devote a lot of time to selecting and monitoring actively managed funds or individual shares. As you gain more knowledge and more experience with the markets, you can include actively managed funds with your tracker funds.

Exchange-traded funds (ETFs) are a type of tracker fund in which the shares are traded on the stock market just like ordinary shares, rather than bought and redeemed through an investment-management company. Management fees tend to be lower than those for a normal tracker fund, so more of the profit ends up in your pocket. If tracker funds interest you, then I recommend that you look at ETFs.

Choosing an Investment Fund

Based on your investment goals, your time frame and the level of risk you're willing to take with your money, you may now have an idea about the kind of fund that may be suitable for you. How do you make a selection from among the many funds that you'll find advertised and promoted online and in the financial pages of newspapers? Here are a few pointers that should be helpful:

- *Consider past performance . . . but take it with a grain of salt.* Visit www.micropal.co.uk, run by US-based company Standard & Poor's, to see comparative past performances of various unit trusts. Look at their performance over a three- to five-year period, longer if possible. Look for consistency. Remember that short-term performance is not a good indicator: last year's winner could be next year's loser. Long-term performance, however, is a more meaningful measure of consistently strong management. But remember: past performance is no guarantee of future results.

- *Check who's in charge.* Some portfolio managers stay with the same trust for years, while others move around fairly frequently. Before investing in a pooled fund, call or visit the firm's website or do research using one of the third-party information vendors to find out how long the manager has been in charge of the trust and if he or she was responsible for the growth that makes the fund an attractive investment for you. One of the important features investors often overlook is the investment adviser's performance during a bear market. Did he or she do better or worse than the average during these years?

- *Consider fees.* For any pooled fund you're considering, check how the fees compare with average fees for that fund category. Hesitate to pay higher-than-average fees, since there are no guarantees that the performance will be strong enough in the long term to make up for the extra expense. In a worst-case scenario, the value of the money invested in the trust may begin to decline.

- *Be sceptical about advertising.* Don't rely solely upon advertised claims to make your final decision. Read the fine print to understand exactly what the fund is (and is not) claiming.

Then do your research to determine the real meaning of the numbers and return. The better you educate yourself, the better the decision you can make.

Investing in a Unit Trust

Investing in a unit trust is quite easy. The size of the initial investment required is usually modest. You can buy the units direct from the company that created and manages the trust or through one of the financial institutions that is an authorised sales agent. Simply telephone the company you've selected and ask them to send you an application form. Alternatively, you can apply online or through one of the fund supermarkets (see Chapter 6), which offer 'one-stop shopping' for many unit trusts and provide you with a quick and easy way to track and manage your entire portfolio of unit trusts.

You can choose to have the dividends from these funds paid out to you or automatically reinvested into the trust. *Dividend reinvestment* is particularly beneficial if you don't need the money to live on, because over time the number of units you own will increase. Units can be bought in a stock and shares ISA. You can make the purchase in either a maxi or a mini ISA (up to a set annual amount per ISA), and you will not have to pay any more tax on gains you have made.

Of course, there are fees associated with investing in a unit trust. These vary depending on the fund. On the typical actively managed fund, there will be an initial charge of around 5% of the amount you invest, plus an ongoing annual charge of 1 – 1.5%. In contrast, some tracker funds have no initial charges, and the ongoing annual fee can be as low as 0.1% of your investment. Thus tracker funds are a bargain.

Obviously the initial and annual fees the unit trust charges will reduce your overall investment profit. For most people, the benefits offered by the trust – especially professional management, diversification and lower entrance costs – make this a worthwhile trade-off. But when choosing a trust, don't turn a blind eye to the fees: they do vary from one trust to another, and those that charge the highest fees are not necessarily the best managed or the ones that provide the best return. All things being equal, look for a well-run fund with low fees and a long history of above average performance. And keep an eye on any changes in the fund's fee structure.

Periodic Investing and Its Benefits

One of the best ways to invest in a unit trust is to have a fixed sum automatically transferred each month from your current account into the unit trust or trusts of your choice. The money is invested before you ever get your hands on it. Depending on your income, you are unlikely to miss the £20, £50, £100 or even £200 you invest every month, and most importantly, you may be delighted to see how your money can grow from dividend reinvestment and an increase in share prices if you've selected a well-managed fund.

A regular premium investment plan allows you to enjoy the benefits of *pound-cost averaging*, a surprisingly simple way of improving your investment profits. When you invest a set amount every month, you actually reduce your average cost per unit. Here's how it works. Let's say you've decided to invest £100 a month in a particular unit trust. Since the price of the units fluctuates as the market price of the shares or bonds in the trust's portfolio moves up and down, some months your £100 will buy more units, while other months it will buy fewer. Over time, you will buy more units at cheaper prices and fewer at higher prices. As a result, the average cost (i.e. the amount you pay) per unit will be less than the average price of a unit over the same period of time. Thus, your profits over the long term are potentially greater.

The table below illustrates the benefits of pound-cost averaging. In this example, the per-unit price varies between £10 and £16 over 12 months. Therefore, the number of units bought each month varies between 6.25 and 10. Doing the maths, you'll find that the average price per unit over the 12 months is £13.08. This is determined by adding up all of the prices per unit each time they were bought and dividing the total by 12 (£156.95 ÷ 12 = £13.08). The average cost, however, is £12.79. It is computed by dividing the total amount of money invested over the 12-month period (£1,200) by the total number of units purchased (93.83). The difference between the average price (£13.08) and the average cost (£12.79) is 29p, a saving of over 2%.

Pound-cost Averaging in Action

MONTH	AMOUNT INVESTED	PRICE PER UNIT	NUMBER OF UNITS PURCHASED
January	£100	£10.00	10.00
February	£100	£12.00	8.33
March	£100	£13.00	7.69
April	£100	£12.50	8.00
May	£100	£11.00	9.09
June	£100	£10.50	9.52
July	£100	£12.50	8.00
August	£100	£14.00	7.14
September	£100	£14.75	6.78
October	£100	£15.20	6.58
November	£100	£15.50	6.45
December	£100	£16.00	6.25
TOTAL	£1,200	–	93.83

As long as share prices are volatile, poundcost averaging always works this way. It's an unexpected benefit of making regular, automatic saving and investing into a habit.

A Final Word

For the average person, unit trusts, OEICs, investment trusts and exchange-traded funds (ETFs) are a great way to move cautiously from the safety and security of saving into the more risky, but potentially more lucrative, world of investing. Don't fool yourself into thinking that there is such a thing as a risk-free investment. (The phrase is one of my favourite oxymorons.) All investments – whether in stocks, bonds, pooled funds or even real estate – involve risk. You need to understand the risk and make sure it is suitable for your investment philosophy. And while millions of people have built and maintained successful investment portfolios that included pooled funds, it does not mean that you have to do the same. However, this investment product certainly deserves a closer look, if only so that you can understand why it may not be suitable for you.

4| INVESTING IN SHARES

Share Investing

As I've explained, investing in a pooled funds is a good way to enjoy many of the benefits of investing while minimising your risks. The pooled funds investor piggy-backs on the expertise of a professional portfolio manager. You also enjoy instant diversification, whether you're investing just a few hundred or a few thousand pounds. For many people, pooled funds are the investment of choice.

Some investors, however, develop an interest in direct-share investing – picking the shares of individual companies themselves rather than buying into a pooled fund's ready-made portfolio. You may want to consider investing directly in individual shares once your portfolio reaches approximately £10,000 in value. If you have less than this amount to invest, it's very difficult to achieve a reasonable degree of diversification.

Make no mistake. Share investing isn't for the lazy or the faint-hearted. Building and maintaining a successful stock portfolio requires time, research, discipline and emotional fortitude. Some people plunge into share investing without proper preparation or the right perspective and lose a lot of money. But those who succeed can enjoy significant profits, in some cases transforming a modest nest egg into a substantial amount of money.

This chapter should help you decide whether investing in individual company shares is right for you. I'll outline some different approaches to share investing and describe both the opportunities and the pitfalls awaiting you in the market. Even if you decide to stick with pooled funds after reading this section, the knowledge you'll gain here won't be wasted. The better you understand how share investing works, the better you'll be at developing investment strategies you can apply to a portfolio of funds . Also, you'll have greater insight into how a pooled fund's portfolio manager makes his or her decision. In short, knowing about share investing will also make you a better investor in unit trusts and other pooled funds.

Buying a Share Is Part of Buying a Company

When you buy an ordinary share in a company, you are actually buying a (small) part of the company. You are entitled to receive dividends – the portion of the company's earnings that its board of directors decides to distribute to shareholders. Dividends are typically declared and paid semiannually. If a company's sales and turnover increase over time, so will the market value of its ordinary shares. If you own them, you would be able to sell them at a profit. On the other hand, if the company does badly or sees its fortunes wane, the market price of the share will decline, generating losses for the holders of those shares.

The most successful share investors are those who know how to analyse a company almost as if they were buying the entire business. Companies with strong prospects for increased sales and rising profits generally make good investments; companies that are losing money or struggling to retain customers and market share are likely to disappoint their shareholders. Thus, one key to the art of share investing is understanding what makes some businesses successful while others fail, and learning to recognise the signs.

Keep in mind that I'm not going to suggest specific companies you ought to invest in. My role is that of financial educator. My goal is to give you a basic understanding of the measures and factors you need to evaluate in order to choose the stocks or bonds that you want to buy or sell. I want to help you become more skilful at helping yourself (or the broker you work with) make better, more suitable investment decisions.

First, let's consider the kinds of companies you might be

interested in as a share investor. One way to categorise companies is by size or *capitalisation*, which refers to the total market value of the company. It's calculated by multiplying the price of one ordinary share by the total number of shares outstanding. The four broad categories of companies based on capitalisation are as follows:

- *Large-cap, or blue-chip, companies* are lwell established companies with long histories of sustained growth. The prices of blue-chip shares are relatively stable and unlikely to move way up or way down suddenly, although of course they can be affected by major news or economic trends. The leading UK blue chips are listed in the FTSE 100. Familiar names there include British Airways, Cadbury Schweppes, Vodafone, Tesco, Sainsbury's and ICI. Many new investors stick to blue-chip companies because of their low volatility (hence they are less risky) and their regular dividend payments.

- *Mid-cap companies* have good products, expanding market share and the potential for above-average growth in profits and earnings. Their prices can rise rise or fall a bit more sharply and unpredictably in response to changes in fortunes. Hence the opportunity for profit is substantial if you pick the right stocks, but so is the risk of loss. Look through the stocks in the All-share Index to find those that fit this category.

- *Small-cap companies* are usually new companies in emerging business areas. Typically their products have captured the attention of the investment market but have yet to establish a strong market presence. Expect the price movement of these shares to be like a ride on the biggest roller coaster in Blackpool. If you pick a winner, you'll make huge gains; if you don't, you'll have heart-stopping losses.

- *Micro-caps* are the smallest and riskiest companies of all. This category includes, but is not limited to, *penny shares* – very cheap stocks that often cost under a pound per share. Don't assume that cheap equals bargain. A better phrase might be 'Cheap is dear.' Many people buy these shares thinking that the prices can't go any lower, and then they do, leaving the investors with losses and regrets. Many of the companies in this group will go out of business, so you must be prepared to lose the money you invest in micro-cap stocks. On the other hand, some people have made huge profits by finding the few companies that do manage to become growing businesses. But the odds are not in your favour.

As you can see, market capitalisation is one of the influences on the amount of investment risk you face when you buy a company's shares. The bigger the company, usually the lower the risk. However, with a larger company, the potential for above-average growth is also less. Here's why: suppose you are running a company with an annual turnover of £10 million. If you can increase your turnover next year by a million pounds, you'll have grown the company by 10%, which is a healthy increase. On the other hand, suppose you are in charge of a company with an annual turnover of £800 million. To achieve the same 10% growth, you'll need to find £80 million in extra turnover next year – a much more difficult challenge for any size of company. This is why large companies tend to grow more slowly than small ones. That usually means less capital growth for investors, but usually less volatility and more dependable dividend payments.

Industry Sectors and Business Trends

Another way of categorising companies is by *sector*. This refers to the industry in which a company does most of its business. You can find a list of industry sectors in the *Financial Times* or on the business pages of your daily newspaper. Important industry sectors include telecom (companies that provide telephone and other electronic communications services), oil and gas, banking, insurance, pharmaceuticals, retail, automobiles, chemicals, entertainment (TV and film companies), packaged goods, aerospace and defence (companies that make military planes, rockets and weaponry) and many others.

The growth and profit potential of a particular company is heavily influenced by the changing economic and business conditions that help or hurt particular sectors. For example, consider the fact that most Western nations have an ageing population – that is, the number of older, retired people is increasing relative to the number of younger, working people. How will this change affect businesses? It seems clear that companies with products aimed at pensioners might benefit. Sectors like pharmaceuticals and healthcare should have good growth prospects in the coming decades as more and more people need products and services provided by these sectors.

Sectors can be affected by unexpected events that cause economic changes. For example, a year with particularly bad weather, earthquakes and other disasters usually causes losses and a decline in the market price of companies' shares in the insurance sector. But such events may be good for companies in the homebuilding sector.

You don't want to invest all of your money in one or two sectors. Remember the principle of diversification: spreading your money among a variety of shares is the best way to minimise the risk to your overall portfolio. Diversifying by sector is an important aspect of this principle. As a share investor, you should follow the business news and keep abreast of the long-term prospects for various industries. One of the best ways to increase the rate at which your money can grow is to identify the industry sectors with strong growth potential for the next five or ten years and buy shares of the best-run companies in those sectors. As these business sectors grow, so will the value of the shares you own.

Sources of Investment Ideas

One of the first and best rules of investing in individual shares is to *buy what you know*. But what do you know? The surprising answer is 'More than you think.' Because you participate in the UK economy as a consumer, shopper and worker, you have your finger on the pulse of certain industries, companies, products and services. For example, many regular customers of the Marks & Spencer retail chain stopped shopping there in the 1990s as the quality of merchandise seemed to drop. Many are now returning as new lines of products have been brought in. Did you recognise this change? If so, you might have watched as the financial prospects of the company fell and rose along with the reactions of consumers.

Think about other categories of goods and services that you, your family and your friends use or buy. Which companies have a reputation for high-quality, well-designed products that lead industry trends? Which bank or building society consistently offers the best products or deals to consumers? Which stores provide the best customer service, and which ones are consumers talking about positively? Which travel agents, airlines, hotels or resorts do you and your friends prefer to patronise? Which brands of toiletries, hair products and cosmetics do you see flying off the shelves? Is there a make of car or electronic product that's on everyone's wish list? Are there particular fast-food shops and clothing stores that the teenagers are flocking to? The answers to these questions can provide a possible clue to tomorrow's fastest-growing profitable businesses, and your next investment opportunity.

Also consider what you know about the industry in which you work. Which companies are expanding, and which are laying off staff? Which companies are well run, and which are seen by those in the know as having problems? Which firm in your industry attracts the brightest, most ambitious and most energetic young workers? Perhaps you can use this kind of knowledge to identify one or more companies that are worth investing in – and others that you want to avoid.

You can also expand your investment horizons by spending a little time every week learning more about a particular industry that interests you. Read the stories on the business pages of your daily newspaper that pique your interest. Listen to the business news reports on your favourite TV or radio station. Subscribe to or pick up one or two of the popular business magazines geared to the general consumer. Start by reading about businesses that affect your life – the industry you work in, for example – or that interest you, like sport, fashion or technology. Read about the companies' new products, marketing and advertising strategies, expansion plans and projected sales growth. You'll find yourself gradually becoming educated about what works in business and what doesn't. This knowledge, in turn, could enable you to see a good investment opportunity that would have otherwise passed by you and your money.

Don't forget that investment opportunities exist beyond the shores of the UK. Today, one can buy shares of companies in the United States and in the emerging markets of Asia, Africa, Latin America and the former Soviet bloc. Many experts predict that growth in the emerging markets should outpace the developed nations of Europe and North America, so it is worth considering investing a small percentage of your money in these markets. You can invest through a global or international fund (perhaps the most prudent option), or you can buy individual company shares with the help of a broker who specialises in overseas investing. Special paperwork and tax forms may be required. Keep in mind, however, that investing abroad has its own challenges and risks. Proceed with caution.

Basics of Fundamental Analysis

Once you've developed an investment idea, you'll want to examine the companies involved from a business and financial standpoint before buying the companies' shares or bonds. The practice of studying a company to ascertain its investment potential is called *fundamental analysis*. Fortunately, it's possible for anyone to learn enough of the basics of fundamental analysis to improve their own share-picking skills. All the information you need is available from a number of convenient sources. What follows is a beginner's guide to analysing a company whose securities you are considering buying.

First and foremost, make sure you understand how the company's business makes its profit. Warren Buffett, one of history's most successful investors, likes to say that he only buys companies that any fool could run, because the chances are good that one day a fool *will* run them. The Buffett method favours businesses with a clear and simple way of making money: the business must be based on a product or service that is unique and essential to a definable group of customers, must have a market that is difficult for competitors to enter, and a brand name associated with quality that attracts new customers as the business grows.

In contrast, many of the Internet-based companies of the late 1990s had unproven business models, small sales and no profits. Yet for a time their share prices soared simply because investors hoped that eventually, somehow, the worldwide explosion of interest in the Internet would translate into huge online markets and enormous profits. Many of the companies failed, and many people who bought their shares lost money. I have a simple motto when analysing companies: if I can't understand the business, then it doesn't mean I'm dumb; it just means that it's not a business I should invest in.

Beyond the basic business concept, however, you need to consider specific data that can indicate promising or troubling financial performance. You can glean most of the information you need from a monthly publication called *Company Refs* (available via post, online at www.companyrefs.com and on CD). It gives detailed financial information on each company it covers along with an opinion about the stock. You can also find some of the same data in the share-listings columns of your newspaper. If you have a broker (as we'll discuss in Chapter 6), he or she will be able to obtain for you detailed reports on any company you are interested in.

Here are some of the items you should understand and evaluate about any company in which you are thinking of investing:

- *The story of the company*. Who started it, when and why? Does it (still) occupy a unique, dominant or distinct place in the market? Is it well managed? What are its plans for the future? Who are its competitors? What kinds of external events could affect its profits? In the future, how quickly are the markets served by the company likely to grow?
- *Turnover and profit history*. *Turnover* is the company's total revenue before expenses or taxes have been deducted; *profit* is revenue minus tax and expenses. You'd like to see that turnover and profits have been growing steadily for several years. If there are any blips in the profit line, you'd prefer that they can be explained by factors like company acquisitions or large investments in new product

development, either of which would increase costs temporarily and therefore reduce profits.

- *Earnings-per-share history*. This ratio is an important measure of a company's health. It's calculated by dividing the total profits by the number of ordinary shares outstanding. If a company is strong, earnings per share should grow consistently. Declining earnings per share may indicate either a problem (for example, declining profits) or a broader malaise in the industry or the economy as a whole.

- *Share-price history*. Every company's share price will experience ups and downs, not all of which are meaningful. You'd like to see a trend that is generally positive (upward) without many extreme swings, either up or down. However, never assume that any price trend is certain to continue into the future.

- *P/E ratio*. The P/E (or price to earnings) ratio is calculated by dividing the share price by the company's earnings per share (EPS). For example, if the share price is £12 and the earnings per share is £0.75, the P/E ratio would be $12 \div 0.75 = 16$. You need to examine P/E ratios in comparison with other companies in the same sector to establish what is a reasonable ratio. A relatively high P/E ratio usually means that opinions about the company's future are very positive. However, it may also mean that the shares are overpriced. A high P/E ratio often goes hand in hand with greater price volatility. A low P/E ratio may mean that the shares are a bargain – or that the company's in trouble.

- *Dividend history*. Check the amount of dividends per share that the company has been paying to investors. Compare this number with other companies in the same sector for an indication of the company's health and profitability. This information is especially important if the dividends from the shares are the source of your current income.
- *Debt* (also known as *leverage*). Compare the amount of debt with that of other companies in the sector. A moderate amount of debt is usually not a problem; it could mean that the company managers have borrowed to buy new equipment or to fund expansion. High debt could indicate a serious problem, since the company will be saddled with large interest payments that may eat up the money it needs to grow.
- *Experts' views*. Check these out, but don't accept them uncritically. The experts are only human and can be taken in by fads, crazes, manias, whims and passing fancies just like the rest of us. It's worthwhile reading their views, but use them as a supplement to your own research, not as the sole opinion you listen to.

Having done some research into one or a few companies that intrigue you, perhaps you're ready to buy the shares. In the next section, I'll explain an easy and risk-free way to test and sharpen your share-investing judgement.

Creating Your Virtual Portfolio

As a special, one-time-only free gift, I'm going to give you £15,000. Don't get too excited – the money is strictly imaginary. You'll use it to buy 'virtual investments' in three companies that you will select, research and track for six months. At the end of that time, you'll have a 'virtual track record' as a portfolio manager. More importantly, you'll have experienced a taste of what share investing feels like – the emotional highs and lows, and the effects of fear, greed and exhilaration on your rational judgement.

'Six months?' you may cry. 'But I want to start with *real* share investing *right now*.' Patience, patience! I'm an experienced share investor, and I always run a virtual portfolio to track shares that I'm interested in for six months before deciding whether or not to buy them for real. Believe me, the losses are *much* less painful when they merely require skipping 'virtual meals', not real ones!

Follow these instructions to create and manage your own virtual portfolio:

1. *Select three industry sectors.* They could include the one you work in, one you have heard is 'hot' and one you would like to learn more about. Make sure they are quite different from each other. (Use the *Financial Times* to find a full list of industry sectors to choose from.)

2. *Pick four companies in each sector.* Choose ones you've heard of, or just choose at random. List your 12 choices on a sheet of paper.

3. *Research all the companies.* Get the relevant page from *Company Refs* (www.companyrefs.com), or from www.hemscott.com. For each company, fill out a share report form, covering each of the criteria I listed in the previous section: the story of the company, turnover and profit history, earnings-per-share history, share-price history, P/E ratio, dividend history, debt and experts' views.

4. *Pick one company from each sector.* Based on what you've learned, choose the three companies that you think will have the best chance of increasing in value over the next six months.

5. *Invest a virtual stake of £5,000 in each company.* Divide £5,000 by the company's current share price (listed in today's newspaper) to figure out the number of shares this money will buy. Round it off to the nearest share. (For the purposes of this exercise, we'll ignore other real-life costs like brokerage charges and stamp duty.) For example, if Company A's current share price is £12.50, you'll divide £5,000 by £12.50. The result is 400 – your virtual holdings of Company A.

6. *Track the price movements of your shares for six months.* Record the share prices of your three stocks on the same day every week. For six months, track how the price per share changes, along with the total value of your holdings in that company, which you calculate by multiplying the price per share by the

number of shares you 'own'. For example, if the share price of Company A increases from £12.50 to £18, the value of your 400 shares will grow to £7,200. That's a £2,200 profit.

7. *At the end of six months, add up your total gains and losses.* What is the final value of your virtual investment? What is your percentage increase or loss? What have you learned from this experience? Perhaps you need to study shares a bit more until you are comfortable with the decision you make?

Just as important as the financial results of the virtual portfolio game are the feelings you experience along the way. Notice how items in the news affect the price of your shares – rumours about mergers, positive or negative information about sales or new products and changes in management can all cause dramatic changes in the value of a company. How do the price swings make you feel? Can you handle the stress when a £5,000 stake dwindles to £4,000 . . . or £2,500 . . . or even less? Do you become giddy when your money grows by 50%, 80% or 100%? Imagine how you'd feel if the money were *real* rather than virtual. Perhaps you're beginning to see why I said that share investing is not for the faint-hearted.

Smart Share-investing Strategies

People who ask me about my share-investing strategies are often surprised to find that I trade very little. For some reason, people assume that being a serious investor means hanging on the telephone or the computer all day screaming, 'Buy!' or 'Sell!' every few minutes to a harried broker at the other end of the line. That's not my style. In 2005, for example, I bought or sold shares ten times all year. Rather than sell shares as soon as their price increases, I have some shares that I've held for more than five years now. They're still doing well and have the potential to do even better . . . so why sell?

I'm convinced that most investors would do well to view themselves as investors rather than traders. (Trading, however, has a sexier, smarter connotation.) Remember that every time you buy or sell a share of stock, you incur transaction costs (more on these in Chapter 6). When you have losing trades, these costs increase your losses; when you have profitable trades, they lower your net gains.

A better strategy is to make your buying decisions with long-term goals in mind. This doesn't mean you should stop checking what the company is doing and how its share price is moving. Stay alert and be ready to sell if any changes occur that make you feel it is time to sell in order to capture your profits or cut your losses.

Here are a few other tried-and-tested strategies that share investors have found effective:

- *Focus on a limited number of companies.* Few people have the time or energy to keep tabs on more than a dozen or so companies spread across a variety of industry sectors. Keep your portfolio simple enough so that you can periodically (weekly, monthly or quarterly) review all your holdings within a limited amount of time.

- *Core and explore* is a good strategy for the conservative investor interested in preserving his or her capital, as it devotes a small amount of money to investing in interesting growth areas. The strategy is simple: put the majority (the 'core') of your portfolio into an established, large-cap fund, like a unit trust, an exchange-traded fund or an OEIC. Use the remainder of your capital to 'explore' investment in individual companies or sectors that are more growth-oriented – such as mid-cap stock or foreign companies. But first, ask yourself how you would feel if you lost your 'exploring' money. Could you cope with the loss emotionally? If not, reduce the amount of money you allocated to the growth part of your portfolio.

- *Follow the company's life cycle.* Most new companies (and their share prices) follow a predictable life cycle. The cycle starts with a volatile start-up period followed by periods of strong growth, then a pull-back as people take profits or the company disappoints shareholders' expectations, and finally stabilisation and gradual growth as the company solidifies its place in the market and successfully implements its long-term strategies. The trick is for the investor to buy in the early phases of the growth period and then sell before the inevitable pull-back. In particular, be cautious about jumping in too early. Companies in the early growth stages are vulnerable to management missteps and get into serious trouble quite quickly. Better to wait until the company is on a more stable footing, even if that means passing up on a portion of the gains enjoyed by more daring investors.

- *Pay attention to market trends.* As you recall, a bull market is a period of investor optimism, when the market as a whole is rising and most companies follow suit. When the bulls are running, buy shares across a broad spectrum of sectors and ride the buoyant market. By contrast, a bear market is a time of pessimism, when most shares drift downward in value. When a bear market strikes, wait on the sidelines and keep your money in cash and short-term liquid securities (as we'll discuss in Chapter 5).

- *Invest over time.* If you come into a windfall, it's probably wise not to invest all of this money at one time. A better approach is to invest a little of the money at regular intervals. As a result, you'll be evening out some of the market's mood swings, which generally produces better profit margins in the long run. Pound-cost averaging, as described in Chapter 3, is another way to benefit from gradual rather than lump-sum investing.

- *Consider using a stop-loss system.* This means establishing a price *below* the purchase price or the current market price at which you will sell your shares. For example, suppose you buy Company M's shares at £18 each. You might decide to set a stop-loss price of £13 per share. (You can instruct your broker to carry out this decision automatically.) Thus, the *most* you can possibly lose on your purchase is £5 per share. The advantage of this system is that it takes the influence of emotion out of your selling decisions, preventing you from holding on to shares as they plummet further and further while you say to yourself, 'Surely it'll turn around soon,' or 'It's certainly going to hit rock bottom by next week.' You might also set a high at which you will sell, or 'take profits'. For example, you could decide that you will sell automatically when the stock reaches £28 per share.
- *Decide to sell the same way you decided to buy.* When pondering whether or not to sell shares, try to forget about what you paid for them and ask yourself, 'Knowing what I know about this company, would I buy these shares today at the current price?' If the answer is no, sell them *regardless of whether you will make a loss or a profit by doing so.*
- *Recoup your original investment and let your profits run.* Once your shares have increased in value, you may want to sell off enough to get back the original amount you invested and

then let your profits continue to make money for you. For example, suppose your original investment of £2,000 in Company R has grown in value to £5,000. You could sell off enough shares to get back the £2,000 you originally paid. (Note: some conservative investors deposit this money into a high-interest savings account.) After the sale, you will still own £3,000 of Company R's shares. If the price continues to appreciate, you'll make money on your profits.

- *Learn from your mistakes.* Whenever you lose money on an investment, don't immediately reinvest the money. Take some time to reflect. Ask yourself what lessons you can learn from the mishap. Did you get carried away and take on a level of risk that exceeded what you were prepared for? Were you dabbling in an industry sector that you didn't know enough about? Did you ignore warning signs because you were overly focused on the gains you believed you would make instead of the possibility of loss?

No one is smart enough or lucky enough to have winning trades 100% of the time. Your goal should be to have more profitable transactions than losing ones. Make a point of learning a lesson from every losing investment and you'll keep getting smarter. You'll be less likely to make truly devastating mistakes.

What *Not* to Do

As important as the investment 'dos' are the investment 'don'ts'. Here are some of my favourites:

- *Don't invest on tips.* One of the most common – and costly – mistakes that novice investors make is to buy shares based on a 'hot tip' from an in-the-know friend, a TV or radio investment commentator, even a complete stranger at a party or on a golf course. These tips are usually based on rumour. And we all know how reliable a rumour is. Always do your own research before you invest your money.
- *Don't buy or sell in response to every market movement.* Don't get caught up in day-to-day price swings. The market's ever-shifting moods frequently do not reflect the true long-term value of shares. Make your investment decision based on the long-term prospect of a share. In short, be an investor not a trader.
- *Don't let tax concerns control your investment decisions.* When you sell shares for a higher price than you paid for them, you must pay taxes on the profits (above a certain level), which are known as *capital gains*. No one loves paying taxes, but some investors allow tax phobia to stop them from selling a security in order to realise profits they've made. This ultimately exposes the investor to risk. If you sit on your gains for too long, you run the risk that the share price will drop and your profits will

vanish. If you think you ought to sell, go ahead and do it – and pay the tax. Paying taxes on a gain is better than receiving nothing on a loss. (Note: it may, however, be worthwhile to *time* your sale to take full advantage of your annual allowance for capital gains tax, currently set at £8,800. Your broker or tax adviser can help you plan such decisions.)

- *Don't buy investments from salespeople who contact you by phone, Internet or direct mail.* High-quality brokers and investment advisers don't cold-call or use other methods of direct marketing to get customers. And the 'incredible investment opportunity' that some direct marketers offer, which 'requires immediate action before time runs out', is more likely to be a scam that will leave you holding a bag of losses. How can a stranger who found your name on some list or in a phone book possibly know your investment objectives, preferences, risk profile and plans? Answer: he can't. So don't respond to the call.

- *Don't get emotionally attached to your shares.* It sounds comical, but some investors fall in love with the companies they own. I've heard people talk about the shares they own as if they were a beloved relative or child. This emotional attachment often causes them to hold on to a stock too, too long, even when it is crystal clear that it is time to let it go because the company is in trouble. Remember, you do not take a wedding vow when you buy the stock. You don't have to hold on for richer and for poorer.

Investing is not a perfect science. And there is no way that all corruption will be eliminated from the market. As I always say in my classes: where there's money to be made, there will always be creative greed, leading a few all-too-clever business minds into grey areas of the law where financial advantage is available. The best advice to investors remains: do your homework, know what you are buying, be realistic about your risk tolerance and don't try to outsmart the market. Finally, when an individual or a company offers a financial return or deal that seem 'too good to be true', it probably is.

5 | INVESTING IN BONDS

Bond Basics

A *bond* is essentially an IOU. When you buy a bond, you are lending money to the government agency or the private company that has issued the bond. In return, they promise to pay you a fixed rate of interest (known as the *coupon*) at fixed intervals (usually seminannually or annually) for a fixed period of time (known as the *term*). At the end of the term, the bond *matures*, and you are repaid the principal or face value of the bond (usually £100). The amount of income that a bond will generate until it matures is predetermined. Hence a bond is referred to as a fixed-income security. In this sense, bonds are different from ordinary shares. When you buy shares, you don't know for certain the amount of dividends that the company will declare and pay because all dividend distributions are at the discretion of a company's board of directors. As a company's fortunes rise and fall, the amount of dividends paid can change.

The Risks in Bond Investing

Compared to shares, bonds are generally a lower-risk investment. Many people think that bonds are no-risk investments. This is simply not true. No investment is completely risk-free. Bonds have some risks that shares do not.

The most important risk to understand about bonds or any fixed-income security is *interest-rate risk*. As interest rates change, the prices of bonds already in the market move in the opposite direction. As interest rates rise, bond prices fall. As interest rates fall, bond prices rise. Imagine that you buy a bond with a 4% coupon rate during a period when interest rates are low. The Bank of England raises its base rate to 6%. Are you going to be happy with your 4% coupon? Probably not. You would probably want to sell the bonds, thus driving the price lower, and buy a new bond with a higher coupon. Also, the market price of the already issued bonds falls, so that the combination of the lower price (called the *discount*) and the coupon represents a yield that is close to the current interest rate of 6%.

A second risk is *default risk*. This is the risk that the company or government that issued the bond will be unable to make the promised interest payments when they are due. Bonds issued by the UK government (also called *gilts*) are considered *almost* risk-free, since the likelihood of the Exchequer going bankrupt or simply refusing to pay off its debts is almost nil. While there is little likelihood that the British government would default on its bonds, the same cannot be said of companies or other governments that issue bonds – Russia and Argentina, for example. To help investors evaluate the risk of default, corporate bonds are rated by an independent agency before they are issued. The lower the rating, the greater the likelihood of default; therefore the company has to offer the investor a higher coupon rate to compensate for the risk. Investment-grade bonds will pay the lowest coupon rate because there is little possibility of default.

In a worst-case scenario, a company, even a large, established one, can go bust. When this happens, interest payments on the company's bonds cease, and the holders of those bonds may lose all or part of the principal they expected to get back at maturity. Under UK law, bondholders generally have precedence over shareholders when the remaining assets of a firm that's gone bust are distributed. This means that when a company goes bust, you'll have a somewhat better chance of getting some money back than a shareholder will. Of course, it's more likely that the company will have no assets left, so even a bondholder could get nothing.

Another type of risk is *inflation risk*. Inflation is the rate of increase in the cost of goods and services, which includes everything from cars and houses to oranges and haircuts. When inflation rises, the buying power (also called purchasing power) of your money decreases. Thus, during periods of high inflation, the market value of bonds declines for two reasons. First, the fixed rate of interest paid periodically by the bond may be lower than the rate of inflation. And second, the principal that you get back at maturity will be able to buy fewer goods and services than it did when you invested the money. Thus inflation would make a bond less attractive to investors because the real value of their money will be diminishing over time.

There are other risks associated with bonds (reinvestment risk, political risk, etc.), but the three above are the most important to understand because they have the greatest impact on the market price of bonds. Despite these risks, bonds remain a popular investment. Investors like them because of two simple facts: 1) you know in advance how much your periodic interest payments will be and 2) you also know in advance how much you will get back when the bond matures. Thus bonds feel and are safer than shares, although they do carry risk.

Government Bonds

Government bonds are called *gilts*, short for *gilt-edged stock*. Every gilt has a *par value*, or nominal value, of £100. That's the amount you'll receive when the bond is redeemed at maturity. However, the market value of the bond will go up and down according to demand, as well as changes in interest rates and inflation expectations.

Gilts are classified by the length of time they have to run to maturity. *Shorts* have less than 5 years to redemption, *mediums* have between 5 and 15 years to redemption, and *longs* have redemption dates of greater than 15 years. Some gilts are *undated*, which means that they have no fixed date for repayment. The government is obliged to pay you interest for as long as you hold the bond, but it may choose to redeem the bond at any time by paying you the par value.

Interest on gilts is generally paid twice a year. *Low-coupon gilts* pay low interest but are issued at a price well below par value, so you'll get a decent capital gain when you sell the bond or hold it to maturity. There are also *index-linked gilts*, which pay an interest rate that varies according to changes in the rate of inflation. The redemption value of an index-linked gilt will also rise or fall as inflation changes, so the return on your investment is virtually free of inflation risk.

The Bank of England produces a useful booklet explaining how gilts work called 'Investing in Gilts' (for a copy, telephone 01452 398 333). You can buy gilts directly from the Bank of England through a low-cost service it provides or through brokers, banks and online fund supermarkets. Make sure you read all the terms and conditions carefully so you understand what you're getting with regard to interest, years to term and capital return.

Corporate Bonds

Corporate bonds are issued by companies when they want to raise capital by borrowing money from investors. Thus the people who buy the bonds are creditors of the corporation. Shares, in contrast, represent part-ownership of the company. The more stable the company, the safer its bonds are likely to be. If you buy a bond issued by a long-established company in a stable industry (a blue-chip company), then your risk is low and the coupon rate paid on the bonds will be relatively low as well. If, on the other hand, you buy a bond issued by a new, small company with little financial history or uncertain financial situation, it will be much riskier and therefore you will be paid a higher interest rate to compensate you for taking on the associated risk. Perhaps you're wondering how the average individual investor can distinguish between more risky and less risky corporate bonds. After all, you're probably not an accountant with experience of analysing the financial statements of companies. Fortunately, there's a simple, reliable source of information about the risk associated with bonds. Several independent agencies, including Standard & Poor's (S&P) and Moody's, study the financial histories, growth prospects, management, financial statements, cash flows and the amount of debt already outstanding of companies that issue bonds, and offer authoritative ratings about the likelihood that the company will be able to make its interest payments and repay the bond's principal on time and in full. Periodically, these services review a company's financial condition and upgrade or downgrade its rating. When this occurs, it is important news in the bonds market and can drive prices up or down.

Although the rating systems vary, Standard & Poor's and Moody's rate bonds on the following scale, listed in descending order, from safest to most risky:

S&P'S RATINGS	MOODY'S RATINGS
AAA	Aaa
AA	Aa
A	A
BBB	Baa
BB	Ba
B	B
CCC	Caa
CC	Ca
C	C
D	D

The first four ratings by either agency are considered to be investment-grade ratings. These are the safest bonds that your money can buy. There is little possibility of default (i.e. the risk that the company that issued the bond will be unable to make the interest payments and repay the capital). A bond rated BB (by S&P), Ba (by Moody's) or lower is described as having significant speculative elements. In short, these ratings indicate significant risk. A bond rated BB, Ba or lower is therefore called a *junk bond* or a *high-yield bond*. A rating of D indicates that the bond is in default. High-yield bonds, despite their attractive-sounding name, are not suitable for conservative investors because the risk of losing all of your investment is significant.

Keep in mind that a bond's rating is not permanent. Recently, for example, General Motors bonds were downgraded to junk status. As a result, many pension funds and other financial institutions were forced to sell the bonds from their portfolio because their provisions prevented them from investing in junk bonds. On the other hand, a young company may get a junk-bond rating when the bond is first issued, but over time, as the company's financial condition improves, it my move up to low-investment-grade status or better. Like all investments, you must monitor the securities you buy because their risk profile and profit potential can change over time.

You can buy corporate bonds through a broker or via your online supermarket (more on this in Chapter 6).

Other Types of Bonds

You sometimes see advertisements in the business pages of your newspaper for various other kinds of financial instruments that are referred to as bonds. These are neither gilts nor corporate bonds but rather investment products, created by insurance companies or other financial firms, that promise to pay a particular return within a fixed period of time. Here's a quick rundown of some of the well-known investments in this category:

- *Guaranteed bonds* are issued by life-insurance companies. They come in two varieties, *income bonds* and *growth bonds*. An income bond pays interest periodically (usually either monthly or annually), and at maturity you'll receive your initial investment back. A growth bond pays you accumulated interest together with the original investment in a lump sum at maturity. With either type of guaranteed bond, your heirs will receive a pay-out if you die before the term is up. There is a degree of risk, in that if you need to cash in the bond before maturity, the amount you'll receive may or may not be equal to the sum you invested.
- *Guaranteed-equity bonds* offer growth for a specified period of time and are linked to a particular stock index, such as the FTSE 100 or the FTSE All-share Index (described in Chapter 3). If the index grows in value, so will your bond; if the index falls, you are guaranteed your original investment back. However, no interest or other income is paid during the life of the bond, so don't choose this investment instrument unless you can leave your money tied up for five

years or so. Guaranteed-equity bonds are offered by National Savings & Investments, as well as by private companies.

- *With-profits bonds* are a kind of insurance policy purchased through a single lump-sum payment. The money you invest goes into a professionally managed fund that may include shares, bonds, cash, even property. There's no fixed term, and you can cash in the investment at any time, although surrender penalties (or market value adjustments as they are called) may be imposed. Your returns will include an annual bonus and perhaps a terminal bonus when the policy is cashed in, both determined by the success of the fund manager in generating investment profits.

New types of financial instruments are being invented all the time, many with the word 'bond' in the title. Before investing, read the description carefully, ask plenty of 'what if?' questions, and investigate the financial strength of the company offering the product. Never forget that 'guaranteed returns' means little if the firm making the promise goes bust after squandering your money.

Bond Funds

As I explained in Chapter 3, a fund is a great way to invest in a diversified, professionally managed portfolio of securities just by writing a single cheque. A traditional *bond fund* provides these same advantages to the bond investor. Rather than trying to create your own diversified portfolio of bonds, it may be easier to buy a well-managed bond fund. The fund manager buys and sells government and/or corporate bonds on behalf of all the fund's investors. The manager tries to generate a good stream of interest income while, at the same time, trying to reduce the impact of interest-rate risk, default risk, inflation risk and other risk on the value of the fixed-income securities in the portfolio.

A junk-bond fund will be more risky. The market price of the bonds will often move significantly in response to changes in interest rates; therefore offering more opportunities for capital gains than a usual bond fund. Remember, however, that the value of the fund can change significantly from month to month. There will be few periods of plain sailing.

Most unit-trust companies offer both a standard low-risk bond fund that offers a relatively low yield with great security and a high-yield fund with greater risk. A bond fund can be purchased in a tax-free ISA wrapper, either in a stocks and shares mini ISA or a maxi ISA. You can invest a bond fund either directly through the fund-management company, through a broker, through a financial supermarket, or through an IFA (see Chapter 6).

Who Should Buy Bonds?

It is probably a good idea for most investors to have some bonds or bond funds in their portfolio to balance the higher risks of any shares they hold. This is a form of diversification. Because bond prices are affected by different market forces from those of stock, bonds offer both greater stability and a *hedge* – i.e. a form of protection – against some, but not all, of the risks inherent in an all-shares portfolio. Here are some other specific investment purposes that bonds can serve:

- A conservative investor who is close to or at retirement age and is primarily seeking a reliable flow of income and preservation of capital rather than building a nest egg for the future.
- A conservative investor who wants to take advantage of the tax-free growth available through an ISA, who wants a better yield than is available from a savings account but who does not want to invest in shares.
- An investor who knows that a set amount of money will be needed at a fixed time in the future may benefit from the security and predictability of bonds. For example, gilts maturing in 15 years can be a good way to finance all or part of a university education for today's toddler.
- An investor who has used the share market to finance long-term goals may want to begin selling shares and moving into

short-term bonds (or cash) as the deadline date approaches.
This reduces the risk that your nest egg will be lost or
damaged by a sudden market downturn with the finish line
looming in sight.

Because they're less volatile than shares, bonds don't get as
much sexy chit-chat as their more risky investment counter-
parts. Some people even seem to think they're boring. Maybe
that's so. But having a portion of your investment portfolio in
relatively safe, predictable, 'boring' bonds can be a huge
comfort during weeks when the price movement in shares
is like riding a roller coaster.

6 | WORKING WITH BROKERS AND OTHER FINANCIAL PROFESSIONALS

What Does a Stockbroker Do?

If you want to buy or sell a *security* (shares, bonds or funds), you will need to go through a stockbrokerage company or through a stockbroker. Even if you place your orders online, they must still go through a brokerage firm. The company or individual broker records the details of your buy or sell order and then routes it electronically to the appropriate market for execution. Once the order is executed, the broker reports the details of the execution back to you, including the amount of money you owe the firm in the case of a purchase, or the money you will receive in the case of a sale. The broker, whether it is a company or an individual, earns a commission for providing this service.

A broker provides other services as well. He or she checks the details of your accounts to make sure they are current and accurate, as well as reviewing the specific securities in your account, the quantities and the amount of your cash balances. He or she makes certain that any dividends or interest paid by securities that you own are correctly credited to your account. And a broker can offer you specific investment advice and suggestions, making sure they are suitable for your financial situation and investment objectives. A good broker can be a valuable partner in helping you to create, manage and increase the value of your investment portfolio.

There are three main types of broker, each offering a different array of services:

- An *execution-only broker* handles the sale or purchase of shares or other securities at your request. The broker receives a small commission on each transaction. An execution-only broker does *not* offer investment advice. Nowadays, the cheapest execution-only brokers offer their services via the Internet and are referred to as *online brokers*.
- An *advisory broker* handles sales and purchases of investments, just as an execution-only broker does. In addition, however, an advisory broker suggests investment ideas and other ways of helping you increase the value of your investment portfolio and achieve your stated investment objectives. He or she should spend time getting to know you – your financial means, your investment objectives, your risk tolerance, investment preference and long-term goals for the money you have invested. Most advisory brokers are

members of large brokerage firms, which provide access to expert analytical information that would not be easy to acquire on your own, such as detailed analysis of the company's financial statements, the overall business in which the company functions, the impact of the current economic cycle and interest-rate changes, as well as the impact of international events. An advisory broker is more expensive than an execution-only broker, but if you take advantage of the expert service and information offered, you might find the additional fees can be worthwhile.

- A *discretionary broker* has written authority to decide what securities will be bought and sold on behalf of his or her client. General investment goals and strategies are set in consultation with the client, but the broker is free to manage the portfolio in pursuit of those goals, making all the daily investment decisions without consulting the client. A discretionary broker's fees are usually a fixed percentage of the total value of the assets under management; however, he or she can also charge a commission per trade.

For most new investors who have little in-depth knowledge about stocks, bonds or funds, an advisory broker is the best choice. Working with a good advisory broker can advance your financial education and open your mind to investment ideas you might otherwise never consider. In years to come, once you've become an experienced investor with a strong sense of your own preferences, trading strategies and investment style, you might consider switching to an execution-only broker and making the investment decisions yourself.

Working With a Broker

The first step in working with any broker is filling out a form to open your brokerage account. The form asks about your financial status, your investment goals, the amount of risk you are willing to accept and where dividends should be paid. The broker will request photo ID (which must be certified if it is a copy) and one or two proofs of address to verify your identity.

You'll also be asked about how you want the shares you own to be held. The most convenient choice is to leave your shares registered in your brokerage firm's official account, called a *nominee account*. By doing this, your broker will be able to sell your shares immediately when you choose. If you keep the actual share certificates yourself, you will have to post them to the broker first before they can be sold. Also, it makes sense to keep money in your brokerage account, so that when you want to buy shares, the transaction can be processed straight away. Otherwise, there may be delays in getting your trade (especially a purchase) executed.

Brokers offer various fee structures. You may be faced with a choice between an annual fee for maintenance of your account combined with a low commission on trades (a worthwhile combination if you intend to make a lot of transactions) or a higher commission on trades with no annual fee (better for those who trade rarely). You will also have to pay stamp duty of 0.5% on every share purchase. When you sell shares, you will pay capital gains tax on any profits (above your annual allowance). These expenses are one of the reasons why it's not a great idea to make too many trades! (The website www.moneyworld.co.uk/trading has a useful table setting out the fees charged by different brokers.)

Know Your Broker

Choosing a broker is a little like choosing a physician. Professional credentials are important, but so are personal qualities. It may take a few attempts to find a broker with whom you're comfortable. It's worth the effort. It won't benefit you to work with a broker who may have a wealth of investment experience and expertise if you find you can't talk openly and honestly with him or her. It is important to find someone who will give you clear, understandable answers to your questions (even questions that some might consider 'naïve' or 'silly') and who will treat you with respect.

You can start your search for a broker by asking friends, family and business acquaintances for personal recommendations. If you draw a blank, the Association of Private Client Investment Managers and Stockbrokers (APCIMS) have a full list of UK brokers (www.apcims.co.uk). Call around and talk with a few of them, first by telephone and then at a face-to-face meeting. I believe it is essential to actually meet the person who is going to work with you and your money.

Record your reactions to each broker you are considering. Pay attention to how you are treated, the tone of voice used when speaking to you, the way he or she listens to and responds to your questions and how each broker makes you feel. Remember, you must have total confidence that this person is interested in working with you and in helping you achieve your financial goals. And you want to know what importance the broker places on giving you good customer service.

When interviewing a prospective broker, it will help you if you prepare the following information in advance: 1) the questions you plan to ask during the meeting (try memorising these so that you can easily include them in your conversation), 2) a clear statement of your short-term and long-term investment goals, 3) any important schedules or timetables that will impact on your financial situation, 4) what kind of risk you believe you can reasonably tolerate and 5) the kinds of investments (blue-chip shares, foreign shares, corporate bonds, gilts, etc.) you think you may be interested in. Below is a list of questions that may not immediately come to mind, but which you must ask any prospective broker.

- Do you handle orders for all of the types of investments in which I am interested? (Note: not all brokerage firms provide customers with the ability to invest in securities that trade outside the UK.)
- What fees do you charge? How do you earn your commission?
- Do you charge an administrative fee for keeping shares in a nominee account and for other services, such as handling dividends? If so, what is that fee?
- Is interest paid on cash held in my brokerage account? If so what is the rate, and how often does it change?
- How quickly will my trades be entered and executed when I place an order?
- How soon will money be released into my account after I've sold shares?

You'll learn as much from the broker's *attitude* in responding to your questions as you will from the answers he or she gives.

Online Brokers

If you are an investor who wants to make your own investment choices and pay the lowest level of commission or dealing costs, then an online brokerage firm is an appropriate choice for you. These companies give their customers the ability to submit buy and sell orders without having to talk to a real person. You, the individual investor, are in total control of your investment decisions. Some online brokerage firms, known as online supermarkets, offer a wide array of investment products, including shares, bonds, unit trusts, etc. Some let individuals manage all their investments, including ISAs and old PEPs, in a single account, thus making it easier to keep an eye on the growth of your portfolio. In essence, an online supermarket is one-stop shopping for financial products. And it makes it easier for you to create and monitor the asset-allocation model that you've established for yourself.

In addition to low cost, online brokers give their customers the ability to place orders from their home at any time of the day or night. Of course, if you place a buy or sell order during a time when the investment markets are closed, your order will not be executed until the market opens for trading the next business day. Once the trade is executed, you'll receive an execution report and can begin tracking the price movement of the securities.

Although online brokerage firms generally don't provide investment advice or recommendations, many supermarkets offer links to research websites where you can read expert opinions about shares, bonds or other investments in which you may be interested or have already invested in. Some will email you with pre-arranged alerts, such as when your shares reach a stop-loss price you selected in advance (see page 85).

As you can see, many tools similar to those available to a traditional, full-service broker are made available directly to the customer online.

Be wary of unsolicited tips and 'hot-stock flashes' that appear as spam in your email inbox or as pop-ups on your screen. Some are sales pitches thinly disguised as independent advice. As most Internet users have discovered, the problem with the sheer mass of information available online is the difficulty of distinguishing between what is useful, what is misleading and what is downright rubbish. That certainly applies in the financial arena. A good general rule to keep in mind is if you don't know who is sending you this financial information, then it's best to ignore it. Do not submit any personal information that can be used to steal your identity or to gain access to your money. Hit the 'delete' button quickly.

Not everyone is psychologically suited for online investing. You won't have a friendly broker or adviser to talk to when prices are falling and panic is beginning to set in. Lacking a human lifeline, some people who invest online end up trading beyond their risk tolerance, either because they are caught up in a fantasy about gains or are desperately trying to recoup losses. The ease and speed of online investing may tempt you to trade more frequently than you would if you were talking to a person. You have to be in control of yourself in order to invest effectively online. To keep a sense of proportion about your investing, avoid falling into the habit of logging on every hour to see what investment prices are doing. Instead, check in at a set time once a week or every other day at most.

Taking Advice

At some point in your life, you may decide that you would like to get help from a financial adviser or investment professional. Most people's finances are relatively simple, and it may be useful to visit a financial adviser to help you establish, then periodically review and adjust your long-term financial plan. Even with today's wealth of financial information in newspapers, magazines, advice columns, newsletters, books and on television, radio and the Internet, most people want some guidance in managing their money, but don't want to feel totally dependent on a professional financial adviser. The trick is to keep your plan simple and clear. This last part is difficult for most people because they tend to see finances as complex: as soon as they begin to earn money, they want to make their plans elaborate.

A financial adviser is worth consulting if you need help in implementing a wealth-building and investment programme; you want to begin investing but are unsure how to get started; you own a number of diverse financial products but lack a coherent investment strategy; or you are worried about your retirement and need advice about how to face a money crisis you don't know how to handle due to accumulated debt, unpaid taxes, divorce, bankruptcy or another emergency.

The first step is to find the right *kind* of financial adviser. Until fairly recently there were two types: an *independent financial adviser* (IFA), who can recommend investment products offered by any company, and a *tied agent*, who sells products on behalf of a single company. But the rules have been changed so that there is now a third type: a multi-tied agent.

An IFA has to be able to recommend products from all the financial companies in the market and must give you the option of paying for an advise by fee. You can pay by commission if you prefer, but you may feel it influences the advise you receive. A *tied agent* can only recommend products from one company and will normally be paid by commission. A *multi-tied agent* is paid in the same way, but will recommend products from several different companies (usually fewer than six).

Generally speaking, a tied agent is useful if you've already done your research and decided you want a product from a specific company. However, if you know exactly what you want, you can often get the product cheaper through a discount or execution-only broker.

As I said earlier, when you're considering hiring a financial adviser, arrange a face-to-face meeting. Bring with you a list of questions and a statement of your financial goals. Don't be swayed by posh offices or smart clothing. Make sure the prospective adviser talks in a way you can understand and offers advice that is truly tailored to your needs. Above all, never be too embarrassed to ask for explanations. The adviser should be able to describe his or her recommendations in language anyone can understand.

Here are some questions to ask a prospective financial adviser:

- Do you deal in all the areas I want advice on? (Some advisers may not handle mortgages, pensions or overseas unit trusts, for example.) Consider whether you want one person to take an overview of all your financial affairs but bear in mind that if so, you may sacrifice expertise for convenience.
- What will your fees be, including both initial charges and ongoing expenses? Is your income based on sales commissions on specific products?
- How long have you worked in this field? (Look for a track record of at least ten years, including experience in both bull and bear markets.)
- Have you had clients with backgrounds and goals similar to mine? How did you work with them?
- What makes you different from other financial advisers? (Watch out for braggarts, individuals who are a little too confident and those who talk only about spectacular or 'risk-free' profits.)
- What qualifications do you have? (Such as CFP, AFPC, AFPS.) Which professional organisations are you a member of?

(Answers may include the Association of Independent Financial Advisers, Chartered Insurance Institute, the Association of Solicitor Investment Managers, the Ethical Investment Research Service, the Institute of Financial Planning and the FSA.)

- How frequently will you provide me with written reports? May I call you with questions and concerns?

Make sure the prospective adviser is asking *you* the right questions as well. He or she should enquire about your long-term goals, your risk tolerance, your timetable and how much you could afford to lose in a worst-case scenario. Be wary of an adviser who seems to offer 'one-size-fits-all' recommendations to every client.

Finally, a crucial word of caution: don't think that hiring a financial adviser means you can fade into the background and just send a cheque whenever your adviser recommends a new trade or security. Working with a financial adviser is not a passive endeavour. You must be involved and informed. Think of your financial adviser as more akin to a personal shopper. It's highly unlikely you would buy a new suit sight unseen without trying it on, isn't it? A financial adviser may have enormous expertise, but he or she should communicate to you why a specific investment or strategy is appropriate for your specific combination of investment objectives and risk tolerance. And you must agree with his or her assessment. Remember, it's your money. Don't relinquish all of the decision-making power to somebody else. And if you are not satisfied with your broker's behaviour or investment performance, leave and find another. Remember, you are not married to your broker – well, at least most of us aren't. And the little bit of embarrassment you feel by rejecting this person may be a small price to pay to find someone new and thereby avoid poor performance or potential losses.

How to Complain

Today, there's no reason to accept shoddy goods, mediocre service or inconsiderate behaviour in any area of your life. I think this is especially true when it comes to the person or place that handles your money and investments. Bad or inappropriate behaviour in this area is often a sign that the company or the individual is taking you and your money for granted. You don't have to put up with this. There is no shame in complaining. It is your right and you should exercise it when you need to. It's not fair to complain, for example, if an investment recommended in good faith by a broker or adviser loses money through unforeseeable circumstances; however, if you have been misled or lied to, you should certainly take action.

Start by writing directly, outlining your grievance and indicating the amount you think you've lost as a result. If you don't receive the remedy you want from the initial letter, write to your adviser's boss marking the letter 'Formal Complaint'. Most companies have a written complaints procedure. If it is determined that your complaint is justified, the company may try to settle the matter internally in order to keep you as a customer.

If you're still not satisfied, you should complain to the appropriate regulatory authority. The FSA produces a leaflet called 'Guide to Making a Complaint', which can be downloaded from their website (www.fsa.gov.uk) or they'll send you a copy if you phone 0845 606 1234.

Join a Club

Another way to learn about investing, to have fun and to profit is to start or join an investment club. A non-profit organisation known as ProShare provides information and advice about joining or launching an investment club. (Visit www.proshare.org for more information.) A typical investment club includes 10 to 20 individuals with roughly similar levels of income and investment goals – family members, friends, business colleagues or simply people drawn together by a shared interest in investing. The club collects money from each member and deposits it in a joint account. Monthly contributions may vary from £20 to £100 or more. The club usually meets once a month. At these meetings, selected members present investment information and ideas. Members usually take turns doing research and making presentations about particular companies whose shares are being considered. Then everyone votes on whether or not to invest. The club employs a broker to handle transactions and maintain records. A percentage of the profits, dividends and interest are shared among the members according to what proportion of the pool each person owns. Typically this money is left in the pool and used for future investment. All investment clubs have rules (based on ProShare's recommendations) governing members, such as how to join the club or how to leave and withdraw your money.

An investment club is a good way of expanding your knowledge about the markets while enjoying an opportunity for socialising. Many clubs meet over dinner or drinks in a favourite restaurant or pub, and some clubs sponsor parties and outings as well as regular meetings.

7| STAYING ON COURSE

Managing and Maintaining Your Portfolio

If you've followed the advice in this book, you've built up your own investment portfolio with a structure and level of risk tolerance you feel comfortable with. You're also investing on a regular basis, putting away money every month with several exciting short-term and long-term goals in mind. Congratulations! You're already several big steps ahead of most people in the race for lifelong security and prosperity.

Now let's consider some ways of keeping your portfolio on course – strategies for managing your investments, boosting their growth and adjusting them to fit in with your changing circumstances over the years.

You don't need to spend a lot of time maintaining your investments. In fact, a little 'benign neglect' can be a healthy approach. Resist checking your share prices and the value of your unit trusts hourly or daily. I recommend noting the share prices weekly. And don't let market fluctuations scare you. Ride out the typical up and down movements of the stock market rather than rushing to sell whenever shares take a dip. Instead, think of down markets as an opportunity to buy shares of solid companies at relative bargain prices.

Devote a couple of hours every quarter to reviewing the overall performance of your portfolio. Consider where you are relative to your long-term goals, and decide whether any specific holding is performing less well than you'd hope. Sell any shares if they've reached the target prices you've previously set.

If you are investing for growth (rather than current income), I recommend reinvesting your dividend payments rather than spending them. Remember the power of compound interest (see Chapter 1). If you let your investment profits contribute to the long-term growth of your portfolio, they'll make an enormous positive difference in the level of wealth you can achieve.

Above all, be patient! If your investment strategy is sound, there's no need to change it because of a bad quarter or two. Most investors will experience occasional periods when they lose money. However, in the long run, most markets can be expected to grow in value, and any well-balanced portfolio should grow as well.

Routine Rebalancing

Approximately once a year, you'll need to look at your entire investment portfolio and decide whether or not it needs to be rebalanced to maintain your desired investment mix. Here's why it's important and how to go about doing it.

As you'll recall from Chapter 2, there are a number of different investment mixes that are appropriate for investors with various kinds of goals, time frames and risk preferences. However, a portfolio that has been set up with a particular mix of shares, bonds and cash isn't likely to maintain that mix over time.

There are several things that could knock your portfolio out of balance. For example, let's say you've decided to use the Conservative or Balanced Mix (60% shares, 40% bonds). Now suppose that the value of your shares in one company increases dramatically over the course of a year. That's good news, but it means that the value of your share holdings has outgrown the value of your bonds. As a result, instead of 60% of your money being in shares, the total might now be closer to 70%.

Rebalancing your portfolio means making buy and sell decisions that will restore the desired investment mix. In this case, you'll want to sell some of the shares that have done so well and reinvest the gains in fixed-interest products, such as bonds or a bond fund.

Don't feel compelled to rebalance your portfolio every time your percentages deviate slightly from the ideal mix you seek. If your 60:40 ratio shifts to 59:41 or 61:39, that's close enough. But if your investments have shifted by five points or more, it's time to rebalance.

Another reason to rebalance is when growth of a single investment undermines the diversification of your portfolio. (As you recall, diversification means owning a range of investments and thereby avoiding the risk involved in having all your money in a single company or sector.) I have a friend who owned shares in a dozen or so companies in a range of industries – banking, electronics, retail and several others. Her portfolio was nicely diversified. Then one of her holdings (a pharmaceutical company) went on a roll; the firm turned out one great blockbuster product after another and enjoyed several consecutive years of record profits. The share value increased accordingly, and in time my friend discovered that the pound value of her shares of this one company had grown to represent 40% of her entire portfolio. This created a happy problem. She was thrilled with the profits, of course, but now her portfolio was dangerously unbalanced: any problems with this company or with the pharmaceutical sector in general could devastate her overall holdings. She rebalanced the portfolio and restored its diversification by selling most of the pharmaceutical shares and investing the proceeds in promising companies in different industries. Thus, she realised some of the huge profits from her successful drug-company investment and set the stage for more years of solid overall growth with an appropriately diversified collection of shares.

Life-Cycle Investing

As you get older, your life circumstances change. Kids leave home, mortgages are paid off, salaries (usually) increase. Sometimes the changes may be more unexpected: a divorce, a job loss or an illness. All such life changes, whether predictable or not, call for a reappraisal of your investment mix.

If you are investing for retirement, you will probably want to change your asset-allocation plan as you get older, moving out of shares (especially those that are more volatile and risky) and into less risky, more secure investments. If you plan to retire at 65, by the time you're in your late fifties or early sixties you may not be able to wait out any stock-market tumbles before you need to begin tapping your investments for retirement income. Consider shifting from the Very Aggressive, Aggressive or Moderately Aggressive Mix into the Conservative or Income Mix (see Chapter 2).

The same logic applies to goals other than retirement. If you are investing for a goal such as homeownership, buying a business or university fees for your children, start moving your money out of high-risk investments and into bonds or cash at least two years before you'll need the money.

As time passes, you should also periodically recalculate how much you can afford to lose. As a rule of thumb, you should only invest money in the stock market if you can afford to lose 20% of it in the event of a market crash or some other mishap. Many people develop a more conservative philosophy as they get older. If you find that your risk tolerance has changed, adjust your investment mix accordingly.

If you receive a windfall from an inheritance, a home sale or a company bonus, and want to use it to expand your portfolio, invest it so as to maintain your diversification and your desired mix of investment types. Consider diversification when selling shares as well. If you decide to sell all your shares in one sector because you think it is set to decline in coming years, research one or more sectors that you're not familiar with and pick a new one to invest in.

Investment Mistakes to Avoid

I was once approached after a book signing by a woman who said she was shocked that, after many years spent explaining finance, I hadn't told people about the 'big secret' to making money. I had no idea what she was talking about. She explained that she had taken a course in spread betting. She was so convinced by it that she and her son had now invested all their money this way, and they were sure they would never have to work again. Taking a deep breath, I explained as gently as I could that 70% of spread betters lose *all* their money. Of course, she didn't want to believe it. I often wonder where that woman is today.

She represents millions of well-meaning individuals who

become impatient with the methodical, careful, step-by-step approach to saving and investing that I've presented in this book. Convinced that the very rich enjoy some secret knowledge that generates endless effortless wealth, they fall prey to hucksters and scam artists selling books, video shows, computer programs, newsletters and telephone tip services that promise to turn small sums into vast holdings practically overnight.

In the next few pages, I'm going to briefly describe some of the most popular forms of speculation, offering just enough knowledge so that you'll understand *why* they are so risky. Not all are equally dangerous, but they belong together because they share the same basic characteristic: all are suitable *only* for investment money that you are prepared to lose in full.

Spread Betting

In financial *spread betting*, you bet on the range of future performance of a stock-market index, such as the FTSE 100, over a three-month period. (This is the form of speculation that the person who approached me at the book signing favoured.) For example, you might bet on the spread of prices in three months' time: if the FTSE 100 is currently at 4,000 and you think the market is going up, you might bet on the spread 4,030–60. If you place an 'up bet' of £5 per point, you would get £5 for every point it rises above 4060 and lose £5 for every point it falls below 4030. Since the FTSE 100 can move as much as 1,000 points in a few weeks, you could lose (or win) some serious money.

Seasoned spread betters try to hedge their losses by betting in two directions at once. However, as with most forms of gambling, the odds are firmly against you.

Futures and Options

Futures and *options* are investment vehicles that originated among traders of commodities – precious metals, oil, cattle, soyabeans, timber. Their initial purpose was to protect companies that used the commodities against future price swings. Today, however, most traders of futures and options use them as a form of speculation. They don't plan to take delivery of the actual commodities but rather will 'settle' the futures or options contract by receiving a payment or making one based on the perceived value of the contract at the settlement date.

Futures and options are now also offered on financial products. Again, the FTSE 100 is an example. In the options market, for example, you can pay a premium for the right to buy or sell shares in the FTSE 100 for a set price within a set period of time. For example, suppose the FTSE 100 is priced at 4,400, and you believe it is likely to rise. You could buy a *call option* at 4,600, giving you the right to buy shares at that price. If the FTSE rises above 4,600, you can exercise your option and buy (for a profit) at that price. If it doesn't, you've lost your money.

Futures and options are valid investment products that play an important role as hedging vehicles for banks, insurance companies and major corporations. However, they're quite complex and highly 'leveraged', meaning that you can lose a lot of money on almost any trade. As a result, the vast majority of individual investors who experiment with futures and options lose their money.

New Issues

New issues are shares in a company that's just joining the stock market. Often, private investors aren't given the opportunity to jump on the new-issue bandwagon. If you are, you may have to send in your cheque in advance with only a vague idea of how many shares it will buy. The company will issue a possible price range, but this is just a suggestion to test demand. If you think the range sounds fair, even at the top end, you send off your money (there's usually a minimum investment) with an application form.

If the issue is popular, you may not get all the shares you want – or even any shares at all – but your money will not be returned for several weeks, during which time it won't be earning any interest.

You also can't predict what will happen to the value of the shares once they start trading. In some cases, the share price might double on the first day if lots of people who applied for the new issues but were unable to get them remain bullish about the company's prospects. Alternatively, if most investors aren't convinced about the company's value, the price could fall sharply when they start trading.

New issues are very volatile due sometimes to to 'irrational exuberance'. In a handful of cases, new issues have created millionaires within a few days of coming on the market. However, research has shown that, over the long term, most people get worse returns buying new issues than they would in a tracker fund. It's not necessary to buy shares in a great new company on the first day they are issued. If the company is truly exciting, it will grow for years to come. I didn't jump on board Microsoft back at the beginning, but its shares have still worked out to be one of my best long-term investments.

Remember that, unless you work in the finance industry, you won't have as much information about a new issue as professional investors and portfolio managers. It's a bit like playing the games in a casino: with luck, you may do well in the short run, but over time the house is certain to pocket the lion's share of the profits.

Art and Collectables

People love to have pictures, sculptures, antiques and other collectable items in their homes just for the sheer pleasure they provide. Wouldn't it be nice if you could also count on serious profits whenever you spend money on such things? It would, but for the average person, art and collectables are better classified as speculative items rather than true investments. Statistics show that most investors in art can expect a return that is less than they would average in the stock market. If you want to buy pictures, choose ones you'll enjoy looking at whether or not their market value grows.

If you're interested in other forms of collectables, stick to the obvious mainstream markets. For example, 30 million postage-stamp collectors spend $6 billion on their hobby every year, according to stamp brokers Stanley Gibbons. But even traditional collectables are quite volatile in price, driven by unpredictable changes in fashion. You might well find a buyer for your collection of Victorian dolls, Art Deco evening bags or Hornby train-set originals, but they might be difficult to sell for the price you want at the time when you most need the money. In the meantime, the cost of insuring and storing them will be eating up your profits.

For an extreme example of human fickleness producing financial casualties, read up on the Dutch tulip craze of 1636. All of a sudden, everyone across Europe wanted these beautiful flowers. With the supply limited, prices rose sky high and fortunes were made. But when the fad blew over, the same tulip bulbs were selling for one-thousandth of what people had paid for them. The flowers were still beautiful, but unwise speculation in their value had ruined a lot of lives.

Property Speculation

In the eyes of many people, an Englishman's home is no longer just his castle; it's also his chance to make big money quickly. A home is not in the same category as a futures contract, a new issue of stock or a painting by an unknown artist. It has an intrinsic value that rarely vanishes altogether, and while you own a house you can at least enjoy the benefit of living in it. Still, housing markets can become dangerously speculative when prices rise excessively, and as I write many financial experts believe that this is happening today, not just in the UK but in many countries around the world.

Many people pocketed significant profits by riding the property boom of the mid-1980s and late 1990s, but many also fell off the ladder during the severe drop in property values in the early 1990s. You'll find plenty of advice about property investing in my book *Climb the Property Ladder*, but here are a few tips to begin with:

- Research local prices before buying. No matter how much work you do on interior design, a two-up, two-down terrace with garden will never be worth much more than other two-up, two-down terraces in the same area.
- Look at lots of nearby properties and talk to local estate agents. Who would the typical buyer be, and what little extras might help to close the deal for them? Do buyers in that area expect an en suite to their master bedroom? Will

replacing shoddy kitchen units generate enough additional money to justify the expense?

- One reasonably low-risk way to profit in property investment is to find a run-down property with potential in an up-and-coming or already desirable area, then do it up. (Of course, picking the right neighbourhood requires good judgement, and renovating a house is hard work, so this can't really be described as an *easy* road to riches.)

- Adding an extra room by converting a loft or building an extension is a good way to add value to your home or investment property. (However, before buying a property with expansion in mind, make sure you can get planning permission from the local council.)

- When doing up a property, keep a good-sized contingency fund; the work will always cost more than you think. Try hard to control the work schedule: the longer the job takes, the higher the interest on your loan will be.

- When planning a property investment, do your sums very carefully. Stamp duty leaps up as you pass certain thresholds, potentially adding thousands of pounds to the sum you have to raise. Remember also that you will have to pay 40% capital gains tax on any profit earned on a house that is not your principal residence. This is going to diminish your profit drastically.

It's very hard to read the property market, even for those who work at it full-time. By the time the newspapers report there's a property boom, prices will have peaked and the smart investor will be selling rather than buying. Can you be sure of buying and selling at the best times?

Don't let me put you off if you want to include property as part of your investment portfolio. Just be prepared to devote a lot of time and money to it. Make sure you have plenty of lower-risk investments in place to offset the risks of property speculation, and don't overextend yourself.

Still Looking for Excitement?

After warning would-be investors about the dangers and difficulties of speculation, I worry that I may be coming across as a wet blanket or a dour puritan out to stifle your personal quest for excitement. After all, there are few things quite as nerve-racking as watching the value of your money swing wildly from profit to loss and then back again, and some people seem to find this activity genuinely thrilling.

If you're in this category, please be assured that I have nothing against excitement. I just hate to see people lose their life savings in its pursuit. If thrills and chills are your primary objective, I suggest riding the roller coaster at your favourite theme park, learning to surf, scuba or skydive, or taking in the latest horror film at the local cinema. Then go home, turn on your computer and watch your savings, invested in well-managed funds, shares of sound companies and high-rated bonds, growing steadily in value. And think about the wonderful goals all that money will help you achieve – a beautiful home, a university education for your kids, a secure retirement and maybe a round-the-world trip or a flashy sports car.

Now *that's* what I call exciting.

Index